More Praise for *Soul Proprietorship*

"Al Killeen's book, *Soul Proprietorship*, delivers a very important tool kit for the development of authentic relationships based on your core values. As a relationship expert, I suggest you use this work to uncover your core values and incorporate them into all aspects of your work and life."

> – **Gay Hendricks, Ph.D.**, Author of *The Big Leap*, co-author
> (with Kathlyn Hendricks) of *Conscious Loving*, www.hendricks.com

"Filled with wisdom, clarity and integrity, Al Killeen's book *Soul Proprietorship* is a blueprint for those who strive to live an extraordinary life."

> – **Andrea Joy Cohen, MD**, Author; *A Blessing in Disguise—39 Life Lessons from Today's Greatest Teachers*, Penguin

"*Soul Proprietorship* offers a pragmatic yet inspired approach to improving one's life—ranging from business interests to interpersonal development. The tools provided are easily worked with and more valuably, presented in such an encouraging way that you want to put them to immediate use. Personally, the strength and confidence that I have gained through Killeen's 'core value' approach has made a meaningful difference in how I live my life."

> – **Bob Webster**, President; Webster Investment Advisors; Director, Western Golf Association and Colorado Golf Association

"Al Killeen's book is the key to personal and professional effectiveness. It is a guide for practicing integrity and truth in daily life."

> – **Greg Osborne**, Senior Executive, Fortune Top 50 Company (client since August 2000)

"You may think you've heard it all, but I guarantee not in the way Al Killeen has put it all together in one place. This is a book about much more than change, it's about transformation."
> – **Jordan Paul, PhD**, Author; *Do I Have to Give Up Me to Be Loved By You?* and *Becoming Your Own Hero*

"This book is a template for sustainable, heartfelt accomplishment, which is the foundation of authentic self-esteem. This is a gift to anyone caring and daring enough to implement the blueprint provided by Mr. Killeen."
> – **Tom Boyer**, Senior Consultant, IMPAQ Corporation

"The Expectations on Leadership continue to evolve. We are under pressure to perform in a rapidly changing, stressful environment, with limited information and limited resources. Having the right tools and processes to overcome these challenges are critical to not only survive but to thrive. Al's got the 'secret sauce' skillfully detailed in his new book *Soul Proprietorship*."
> – **Daniel R. Meyer**, Founder, Global Wealth Strategy Partners, LLC; Registered AXA Advisors

"The message of this book is so encouraging because it reflects the life work, heart, and personality of one of the most encouraging individuals that I have ever met. Since my introduction to Al Killeen, my life has been characterized by a relentless pursuit of opportunity. Al called me to a bigger game in every aspect of my life, and then gave me the faith in myself to play that game. The contents of this book can encourage you and give you the faith in yourself that you need to play that bigger game, and the richness of life that flows from it."
> – **Michael Watkins MBA/JD**, President, Guild Associates, LLC (client since 2002)

Soul Proprietorship

8 Critical Steps to Overcoming Problems in Business and Life

Al Killeen

Be your Gift!

Al Killeen

Mason Works Press
Boulder, Colorado

Al Killeen would love to hear from readers. Please email him at alk@IntegrativeMasteryPrograms.com and visit www.IntegrativeMasteryPrograms.com.

Disclaimer: While the publisher and author have used their best efforts in preparing this book, they make no representations or warranties with respect to its accuracy or completeness. In addition, this book contains no legal or medical advice; please consult a licensed professional if appropriate.

First Edition

Edited by Stephanie Roth and Melanie Mulhall
Cover photograph by Al Killeen
Cover and Interior Designed by Nick Zelinger

Library of Congress Control Number: 2009937058

ISBN 978-0-942097-26-9 (paper)
ISBN 978-0-942097-25-2 (hardbound)

Printed in United States of America.

ACKNOWLEDGEMENTS

It is with deep humility that I acknowledge all of the sources for the material in this book. Thanking everyone involved is impossible as the information comes from forty years of personal inquiry and learning from countless people, both directly and indirectly. The following are who I can thank, and I beg the forgiveness of any who are not named. Please know that this book is sourced from you through my articulation of your knowledge.

Thank you to:

- God and all the Angels, Saints, Saviors and Holy Ones, for their eternal guidance.

- My wife and life partner, Reese, for her inspiration and faith.

- My sons, Cameron and Holden, for teaching me to be more principled than egocentric (because with kids, you have to be the message whether you want be to or not).

- My extended biological family for companionship through this brief, yet eternal journey.

- My clients, for the enlightenment and vulnerability to truth.

- My friends, for support and belief in me when I have so often lacked it.

- My various business partners, for all that they have taught me, both comfortably and not.

- Inspirational strangers who have validated belief in the ocean that we are all a part of.

- All the wise ones who have written what I have read and shown me the various paths up the mountain of awakening.

This book is dedicated to
Reese, Cameron, and Holden.

To live a life of great Success requires mere effort;
To live a life of great Significance, however, requires great personal purpose;
Success doesn't necessarily lead to Significance,
but Significance always leads to Success.

Al Killeen, President, IMP

FOREWORD

There are quantum leap moments in thought and action, whereby qualitatively profound truths are presented across the centuries. In these instances, we are reminded by a few Masters of the essential, most basic, and core ingredients necessary for the survival of mankind. Buddha, Jesus Christ, Mohammad, Lao Tzu, Saint John of the Cross, Gandhi, Martin Luther King, Jr., the Dalai Lama, and other inspired, like minded thinkers have momentarily changed our world with their messages of love, peace, hope, respect, communication, and tolerance.

Scientist, spiritualist, and physician Dr. Deepak Chopra tells a story of a 13 year old girl who in the act of meditation, can call to the whales near her home, and they respond by coming to her. When asked by an awed spectator how she performs this feat, the young girl simply replied that she merely goes deep inside herself, to that place where "we all speak the same language." Unfortunately, as a species of *homo sapiens*, connected with all interplanetary and sentient beings, we rarely go to the place inside ourselves where we all speak the same language. Instead, the "isms" become prominent: egocentrism, sexism, genderism, racism, ageism, nationalism, "religionism." And what is this common language that we all speak? You already know. Deep inside of you. It is the language of love, kindness, compassion, gratitude, appreciation, acceptance, forgiveness, respect, and tolerance.

As a planet and species, we now find ourselves faced with the horrifying end-game concepts of multi-continent wars, human caused climate change, mass extinction of the world's native species, starvation, and overpopulation of the planet. A Buddhist sage once commented that all wars start with a search for bread. Where will it end? Stated simply, will humanity still exist as a life form on the planet Earth next year or in the twenty-second century?

As spiritual beings engaged in daily human experiences, it is critical that we be in a constant state of evolution, or we wither and die intellectually, physically, globally, and spiritually. Ongoing change occurs in the arts, fields of science, technology and medicine, and spiritual philosophies. However, many other areas have remained more impermeable to change, including the way we treat other creatures on our planet, relationships with our neighbors, personal belief systems, and the business arenas. This insightful book by author and life coach Al Killeen addresses these critical areas of manifesting personal, business, community, and global transformation.

Al Killeen has magnificently unveiled a lifetime of reflection, introspection, creative insights, and wisdom into this beautifully crafted, cutting-edge work, which concisely presents his eight steps of personal, business, and life transformation. Killeen masterfully takes the reader through thousands of hours of business coaching to instruct us in the ancient and contemporary wisdoms of self and global transformation, in logical step-by-step sequencing. He builds off the premise that one must first develop a mindset of honoring the self and spirit as a key to psychological, business, relationship, and spiritual growth.

More than just another "how-to" book of personal development, Killeen presents the revolutionary concept of constructing a genuine transformative core based on a personal life vision that is held onto throughout all events of living. I strongly encourage you to take the time to develop your own personal life vision, using the process he outlines, to create the foundation you will need for the remainder of the steps. The time you take to do this will be richly rewarded.

This transformative process embodies both personal and integrative global changes. The author interjects moving personal experiences into the book, with a delightful ability to blend numerous other wisdom traditions with his own wit, humor, ingenuity, and creative enlightenment. Rather than presenting himself as "the expert," Killeen's stories show he is learning the same lessons he is asking you to learn, while demonstrating his fallibility as a businessperson, a father, and a man. What makes his book so engaging is his premise that he is in the trenches with us, holding our hands and guiding us, while at the same time leading the way. This "been there, done that" approach helped me see that the time it takes to go through these steps will be well spent.

I am confident you will find this book to be a compelling read if you are interested in business, coaching, spirituality, philosophy, and psychology. I feel it is a brilliant, must read for those on the path of enlightenment in broadening their spiritual and business cores in the twenty-first century.

Allen D. Brandon, Ph.D.
Founder, Rocky Mountain Neuropsychological Sciences, P.C.
Fort Collins, CO 80525

CONTENTS

INTRODUCTION

You are what your deep driving desire is;
As your deep driving desire is, so is your will;
As your will, is so is your deed;
As your deed, is so is your destiny.
—The Upanishads

Everyone faces problems in every domain of his life at some time. Many people have an intimate relationship with adversity, which seems curious because we are basically creatures of comfort. We design our lives to maximize our comfort and minimize our discomfort.

When problems do arise, however, it is great to have a way to work through them—a proven, time-tested method. That's what this book gives you: eight critical steps that a person, organization, or team can employ to overcome problems in business, relationships, and life as a whole.

The eight steps are presented here in a linear fashion and should be read in the order presented. However, in using the steps to solve problems, you may find that you need to jump from one to another to be effective.

In a team or organization, dialogue and communication must take place and all eight steps should be discussed before beginning a project. It may take time to go through the steps, but doing so will create a collective sensibility among the people involved and you will craft a beautiful solution that will be easily executed. In thousands of hours of coaching executives, I have seen these eight steps guarantee movement toward positive resolution.

For an example of how these steps ensure victory, consider Ernest Shackleton[1] and his Imperial Trans-Antarctic Expedition of 1914-1917. They never made it to the South Pole but, over many months, their ship was frozen in the ice and crushed, they were stuck on the ice, they survived an open water voyage, yet Shackelton brought all his men home alive. How?

- He had to have the right mind-set (Step 1).

- He had to be objective about where he was starting from and the reality of his situation (Step 2).

- He had to remember the goal of survival and have faith that they could survive (Step 3).

- He had to have a plan to keep people occupied and productive (Step 4).

- He needed to notice where barriers arose and what breakthroughs were possible regarding his people's thoughts and emotions (Steps 5 and 6).

- He made sure that he and everybody on the team was committed (Step 7).

- He monitored people constantly to make sure everyone executed commitments (Step 8).

Welcome to the exploration of these eight critical steps. I am excited for you. This template will grow your life, help you manage and overcome problems, and amaze you when you see what you can achieve with the right mind-set and tools.

---

[1] See *Shackleton's Way: Leadership Lessons from the Great Antarctic Expedition,* by Margaret Morrell and Stephanie Capparell.

An Overview of the 8 Critical Steps

Here is a summary of the eight steps you can use to solve any problem in business, relationships, or life as an individual or a team.

Step 1: Mind-Set

Establish a mind-set based on your core values, not on the comfort of your past scripts or personality preferences. This empowers you to make more objective and effective decisions that will more naturally appeal to other people involved in the situation or problem.

Step 2: Current Reality Analysis

Analyze the problem from an objective perspective, in terms of "effectiveness" rather than "right or wrong." Look at what is working and what is not working right now. Depersonalize and review it completely.

Step 3: Inspired and Desired Future Outcome

What is the best possible outcome to solve this issue? Don't think about how to get to the solution. Simply allow yourself to envision the optimal outcome from a broad perspective.

Step 4: Process for Moving from Current Reality to Desired Future Outcome

Create the road map to resolution and the milestones of progress toward realizing your inspired vision. Identify the action steps you will take to reach the milestones. Identify who will execute the action steps.

Step 5: Barriers to Executing the Process

Identify what barriers could obstruct your progress. Do you have personality traits that could stand in the way? What external factors might inhibit the process?

3

Step 6: Breakthroughs to Barriers
Identify how you will break through the barriers.

Step 7: Commitment to Executing the Process
Are you and the others involved truly committed to executing the process? Are you willing to experience the potential discomfort of operating effectively to resolve the problem as an expression of your core values? If so, proceed. If not, what must you do to gain commitment?

Step 8: Follow-Up Monitoring System
Identify how you will measure progress and ensure effective execution of your road map.

These steps are interdependent. All must be included if you hope to realize your desired future outcome.

How This Book Came To Be

I have taken nine years to write this book. It has emerged from a yearning for connection. In those nine years, I created a new business and captured an eruption of thoughts that have been percolating within me for nearly forty years.

We wander in and out of careers, relationships, and communities with the hearts of minstrels, the minds of students, and the hopes of young lovers on a quest to make sense of it all. Yet, the answers somehow elude most of us.

This book is my humble attempt to dislodge the answers from their rocky and remote domains, and I hope you find the approach refreshing. It comes with an outrageous premise: If your life is more extraordinary and fulfilling after following this guide, I will know this book is successful. That is why I wrote it.

This book is meant to be unlike anything you have ever read. It is an authentic offering of the best of my heart and mind and is intended to provoke the best of your heart and mind to awaken your great gift.

Your gift is the unique place within you that wasn't here before you and won't be here when you are gone. Your gift is something important for you to understand because that understanding will unleash your mastery and begin to awaken power in other people's lives. The reason we are here is to find the code that unlocks our personal mastery and the path for accessing it.

How To Use This Book

Your best approach to this material is this: Make your own rules. Take one or more of the following approaches:
- Read it from start to finish like other books.
- Review the Contents and read any title that intrigues you.

- Let the book fall open in your hands, find the nearest chapter heading, and begin reading.

I recommend that you read no more than one chapter at a time. Give yourself time to think deeply about the message of that chapter and your answers to any questions asked. Use the concepts in each chapter to guide you to a new perspective. You will find greater impact and enjoyment if you are patient and let each chapter provoke you to deeper answers within yourself. I suggest you start a journal to record your journey and answer the questions we pose.

Finally, consider that this book may lead you to answers that provoke solutions for all domains of your life. These domains include:

- Career and Business
- Relationships
- Family
- Health
- Intellectual
- Creative
- Spiritual
- Others you define

The tools of personal mastery are universal in their application and valuable to all domains. Whether you are a business owner or manager who wants to improve performance, or a parent who wants to help your daughter find her way, you will find the answers in these pages.

Direct vs. Indirect Living

This book is designed to help awaken you to thoughts and ideas that will change your life. One place to begin is to notice how others are living and one measure is "direct" vs. "indirect."

As you start watching people, you will notice that 98 percent of the people around you are living life indirectly and only 2 percent are living directly.

When you live indirectly you:
- work forty to sixty hours per week at a job that doesn't fulfill you or match your core values and you don't leave because you need the money to "survive"

- wait for weekends, evenings, or retirement to live how you really want to—anything else would be "irresponsible"

- would like to trust your talents, passions, or core values to guide your life, but your résumé, history, and experiences seem "safer"

- live fearing what might happen instead of committing to what might happen

When you live directly you:
- identify your core values, passions, and gifts and use them to design your life

- identify your priorities and spend as much time as possible manifesting them

- align your core values, passions, personal talents, and envisioned future with a pathway to fulfillment—and live a fulfilling life

Are you living life indirectly or directly? How? Why? What will you do differently from this point forward?

Comfort vs. Commitment

I hope you become uncomfortable while reading this book and doing the exercises. Why? Because most of us cruise through life with the goal to stay warm, safe, and dry. The worry alarms are off. You have enough money for now, enough love to avoid facing yourself, and enough acceptance to avoid looking in a clear, dust free mirror. You are pretty comfortable.

Then, suddenly, you sense the presence of your brilliant possibility, a nagging voice of what your life could be. It begs for your attention and asks you to consider another future. It asks that you not settle for warm, safe, and dry. It asks you to remember what it felt like to be whole and how it might feel to be fully alive, more than "not dead."

You constantly face competing commitments, largely unconscious, largely unrecognized. You hide them from others, like something you cannot discuss or share without exposing your humanness.

Not knowing what others would think, you defer to the path of least resistance, your past scripts, your comfort zone. You choose the mediocrity of your past over the siren call of your potential. You settle.

Instead, you could choose to courageously act toward what you want. You could choose self-faith and resolve over self-doubt, timidity, and fear.

This book will help you make the choice to commit to what you could be.

Sources of Personal Power

Personal power is an ongoing and repeated premise of this book. It is based in your identity and begins with the thought that you can choose your identity. That choice is between your ego and your values.

Most people think that they are their ego, their physical entity that grows, lives, and dies with their body. But what do people talk about at funerals? Values—the personal principles the life represented.

The impact people have is how they express their values and principles through their life decisions and actions.

Two Sources of Personal Power

The first source of personal power comes from shifting your identity to your values by asking questions like, "What would my value of integrity or honesty do right now?" instead of, "What is comfortable for me?" or, "What would my ego do?" When you do that, you actually gain strength and support from the Universe to operate courageously and effectively.

The second source is to work with time in your perspective. You can be in the moment (values or power), or you can project fear forward or regret backwards (ego or disempowerment). Disempowerment creates paralysis and self-protection. Instead, when you operate from your values, you operate more courageously.

When you operate as an expression of your values, you access the power of the Universe.

Now Is Your Time

I watch two types of animals near my office building: rabbits and foxes. The rabbits spend their days paralyzed by fear. They huddle, frozen, and await the hungry fox who hunts them. The fox hunts with purpose and diligence. He knows that if he does not catch a rabbit, he and his kits will go hungry.

Today's world news invites you to be a rabbit, but you have the power to be a fox. If you resolve to be a fox, you will grow fat and happy and take care of your children—and maybe even teach the rabbits how to become foxes.

Here is how you might do that:

- You get what you focus on in life. If you focus on fearful outcomes, you will create them. If you focus on positive outcomes, you grow and flourish, even in times of adversity.

- Be persistent. My father-in-law started and failed at twenty-five businesses over twenty-five years. The twenty-sixth business made him wealthy. He learned not to take setbacks personally. Instead, he learned from them and kept trying until his consistent and bold commitment finally gave him freedom, options, and economic independence. Be resolved to do the same.

- You trade your "value proposition" for compensation. It consists of price, actual value, and perceived value. If you focus on price, you may lose out to larger and cheaper offerings. If you offer actual value without concern for price or perceived value, you may end up bitter and alone with the sense that the world didn't recognize your value. If you offer only perceived value, your customers abandon you when it does not match actual value. Therefore, the secret to success is to first pay attention to perceived value, then authenticate it with actual value. This is also known as "under-promise and over-deliver." You create a highly valued offer that grows more as time goes by.[2]

- If you watch the nightly news or read the daily newspaper you may feel great fear and despondency. Or turn off the news and stop programming yourself into a mind-set of fear. Take control of the one thing you actually can control: your frame of mind.

---

[2] Example: You may perceive a Lexus automobile as valuable. That perception is backed up by its actual value. If you buy one, you own it for a long time because of its quality. Therefore, it becomes a better value over time and costs you less than a cheaper car that is not built as well.

- You may have lost a substantial amount of your net worth during downward trends in the stock market and housing market. Get over it. Create it again—bigger and better— with the wonderful gift of wisdom gained from your experience. Life involves risk, and your "net worth" is not what you have in the bank anyway. Your true material wealth is in what you can and will produce in the future. As Warren Buffet says, "Be fearful when others are greedy, and be greedy when others are fearful."

- Don't focus on the current reality of problems as much as the future vision of what you want. If you focus on what is not working today, you will be stopped or paralyzed. If you focus on where you are inspired to go, you invite the Universe to open doors for you in remarkable ways. You get what you focus on, good or bad, so be a jealous guardian of your focus.

- Help others. There is no greater way to take control of your own life than by supporting and contributing to others. This may seem like so much sugar water of motivational moralizing, but it is an actual path to power. When you focus on benefiting others, you not only create good "karma" and outcomes, but you forget to diminish yourself with self-defeating thoughts or activities that keep you from productive action.

- What you believe about yourself, the world believes about you. You will truly believe great things about yourself when you get crystal clear on your core values (see page 28) and personify them. Then, notice how others begin to believe in you in a dramatically greater way. They will respond by awakening their own values as you invite them into a far more loving and empowered relationship.

- The Chinese character for wealth is composed of two symbols, "trade" and "brilliance" (in the sense of your unique brilliance in life). When you create a value proposition that trades in your unique brilliance or gift in life, you become irresistible to others and eventually create great success.

- Concept + Experience = Ownership of Truth. These truisms won't do anything if you don't immediately try them out in your life and work today. Otherwise, they will fade into memory and you will be drawn back into the fear of the rabbit. If you experience them, you will see their truth and find the world far brighter, because you are.

Go out as a "Warrior of Light" who shines that perspective into the world. It will help eliminate your fear and create purposeful and effective action in your life and others. The rest of this book will help you do this effectively.

The Empty Cup

A reporter from New York City goes to Japan to interview an old Zen monk who has been in the monastery for forty years. The reporter thinks the monk has wasted his life meditating and raking rocks—whatever he does in the monastery without women, wine, or song.

He asks question after question, barely letting the old man talk. The monk eventually calls for tea. When the tea comes, he pours himself a cup and then pours a cup for the reporter, who continues to yammer on with his incessant questions.

The old man starts to fill the reporter's cup. When the tea reaches the top of the cup, he keeps pouring. It pours over the edge, onto the table, and eventually off the table and onto the reporter's lap, which causes the reporter to jump up and say, "You crazy old man, what are you doing? Why did you do that?"

The old man says, "Your mind is like that cup. If it is full, I cannot put anything in it, just as I cannot put any tea in the cup when there is tea already in it. Empty your cup and then I can put something in it."

Shunryu Suzuki, who introduced Zen to America, said "In the beginner's mind possibilities are many, but in the expert's mind possibilities are few." We have to be able to empty our minds and become learners, rather than knowers, to expand ourselves and grow. Otherwise, we spend a lot of time simply validating what we already know.

When I feel my mind is overly busy, I go to bed at night and turn a cup upside down on my bedside table. When I wake up in the morning, I notice the cup and turn it over as a reminder to have an empty cup as I go through the coming day.

As you read this book, have an empty cup. When you are done, see if there has been some shift in you. Don't lock it out by trying to defend that which you already know.

Beyond Warm, Safe, and Dry

Earlier, we talked about comfort vs. commitment and being warm, safe, and dry. As you grow, your needs begin to shift. Eventually, at age thirty or forty or fifty, you decide to grow up.

Many of my friends and clients are getting in touch with those shifting needs. Rather than maintaining the status quo (that warm, safe, and dry feeling), they want more from life. The drive for true meaning in their lives becomes paramount, and the courage to find it begins to supersede the relative boredom or stress of mere survival.

Sometimes this search is catalyzed by a life event that causes upheaval. You lose a parent or a job, your spouse decides to leave, the kids move out. Whatever the cause, more and more people are less willing to settle for mere maintenance. They are demanding lives that matter.

My wife has a piece of stained glass that hangs in our laundry room. It says, "Your life is a gift from God; what you do with it is your gift back to God."

People want to use their personal life gifts in significant ways so they can feel they are spending their lives appropriately and not wasting them. Do you ever think about moving beyond safety and security and getting to real fulfillment in your life? Is your current career worthy of you? Is your family life as fulfilling and creative as it could be? Do you work on your life from an empowered and inspired place, or do you use fear as your motivator to stay warm, safe, and dry?

These are some of the issues you can use this book to sort out. Although they may seem like philosophic journeys to get to "when I have time," isn't now a great time to start looking at these deeper issues?

Your Life as a Gift

My father lived to age ninety-five. He was a wonderful human being, healthy right up to the end. And he felt he had wasted his life because he had spent it as a child of the Depression, trying to play it safe, carefully avoiding the discomfort, fear, and survival challenges he'd had when he was young.

As a result, in his eighties and nineties, he expressed regret over how he had spent his life. He had worked in government for forty years and had been married for fifty years, much of the time spent unhappily in both relationships. He had played it safe, not wanting to lose what he had, whether or not he was happy with it.

Your life is a gift. What you do with it is your choice. Why not be bold? Don't waste a single precious minute. Use this book to help you begin to make new choices and bold moves.

∽o∾

STEP 1
Mind-Set

To laugh often and much. To win the respect of intelligent people and the affection of children. To earn the appreciation of honest critics and endure the betrayal of false friends. To appreciate beauty, to find the best in others. To leave the world a bit better, whether by a healthy child, a garden patch or a redeemed social condition. To know even one life has breathed easier because you have lived. This is to have succeeded.
— Ralph Waldo Emerson

Many people are confused about the difference between "mind" and "brain." Much of the English speaking world lives in a linear culture that sees things in black and white, yes and no. We want everything in logical, left brain data, so "mind" is often synonymous with "brain."

When viewed from an Eastern spiritual and cultural perspective, the mind is actually much larger than the brain. I use the largest definition of mind, one that goes far beyond the brain and our rational abilities. Mind spans the whole canvas of your knowing ability— your cognitive, psychological, physiological, emotional, intuitive, and spiritual understanding. Mind-set is important because it includes the whole ocean of consciousness with which you look at a situation.

This book discusses the eight critical steps for solving problems and overcoming barriers and challenges in your life. Mind-set helps establish an environment that is as large and complete as possible, one that gives us many options to:

- analyze where we are and determine where we want to go
- see obstacles to break through them
- exercise discipline to create your journey and execute it

Starting as Big as Possible

From Greco-Roman times, Western civilization has developed into a linear society that worships rationalism, believes the world can be viewed objectively and controlled, and clings to the need to be "productive." The "self" that has adopted this mind-set closely aligns with the smallest level of identity, the ego.

We believe we are individual drops in an ocean of other drops. If we see ourselves that way, we operate that way. As Maslow captured in his hierarchy of needs, safety is the second most basic need of an individual. Only physiological needs rank lower.

If your mind-set is limited to the shallow ego identity, its natural tendency is to analyze the current reality, the future, and a road map to that future in the same way. At the other extreme, if you approach a situation from the identity of the entire ocean—from your eternal nature or larger self—your perspective is that everything in the Universe is available to you. You can use that larger view to analyze where you are, where you want to go, and how to get there.

If this sounds esoteric and philosophical, bear with me. You will ultimately see its practicality.

An individual can realize that he has a choice, perhaps for the first time, about his identity. Why does one's identity matter? It matters because when you choose your identity, you determine your mind-set.

For example, if my identity at a given moment is to be a manager, I operate as a manager. However, if I choose not to be a manager, or even an individual ego, but instead choose to become a living expression of my values, then I approach the situation from a larger and more spacious perspective. Let's get specific.

In my role as a manager, I have an employee with a problem. I am thinking as a manager, so I access my mind's database of what good managers do. I may think about what Tom Peters did in the seventies or what my favorite boss did or didn't do. I may think about what I should have done or what I could do differently.

All these thoughts, through the role of a manager, help me access that data intellectually, intuitively, and spiritually. They tell me what a good manager does, which may or may not be consistent with my usual way of behaving. If my employee made a mistake and I operate as a "good manager," I may choose to discipline or coach her. I do this from a managerial standpoint, with my ego persuading me to fulfill a traditional managerial role.

But let's say that I operate from my core values, which I have captured in my Personal Life Vision[3], instead of operating from my role as a manager. Now I can ask myself what integrity would do at this time. I see the situation in a bigger context, and realize that she is going to make mistakes in her life. I act with integrity or honor rather than with what simply makes me feel good as a manager.

How will she react to this "new" manager? She will react to "integrity" rather than "manager." The integrity solution will always access a larger set of timeless and universal principles.

Life is basically a mirror. If I operate as an ego, even with the best of intentions, my role as manager will create a reaction in my employee that is the reaction of one ego to another. However, if I operate from a specific value, then I invite her to also operate from

---

[3] "Personal Life Vision" is a concept further explored and defined later in this book.

that value. If I operate as integrity, she may also operate as integrity. If I operate as anger, she may also choose to operate as anger.

Expanding Mind-Set

Mind-set is about determining how you will look at a situation, using your largest possible self and the biggest repertoire of data, to find the possible futures that can be generated from it. Mind-set produces the context for response and proactive creation. It is the first critical step in the problem solving process.

If you stop in the face of a tough situation and hesitate long enough to look at your core values and your personal life vision as the context for response, I guarantee you will have a much better outcome than if you respond in the knee-jerk fashion of your ego. The animal in us wants us to operate from ego, but the Divine in us invites us to use this more sophisticated, subtle, and valuable approach to analyzing situations.

So the question with mind-set is: Will you give yourself the opportunity to remember that you are a part of God rather than merely an individual entity trying to survive this situation?

Will you operate from your largest mind and not just your small, reactive ego brain? Your mind-set changes everything. This chapter is designed to start you thinking about your mind-set.

As you work through the exercises in this chapter, remember this idea of mind-set to determine what you really want. Look at the balance in your life, start to strategize your personal life vision, and see where your mind-set is operating: ego or values.

What Do You Really Want?

Do you make New Year's resolutions? Are they posted on your refrigerator? Have you written down your business or life plan for the year to come?

Most people write them down and even start out strong. Then, "just this once," they stop executing the plan. One excuse leads to another, then another, and pretty soon that plan disappears completely. Like bottles floating out to sea, they never seem to get back to their great intention.

Sound familiar? Does it seem more acceptable that you do this when so many other people do the same thing? Do you notice how quickly the years go by and how the great things you intend to accomplish never seem to happen?

It's not too late to change.

Why People Fail

Most people fail to achieve their goals because they set them from scripts based on the past or on reactions to life's circumstances. For example, let's say you are overweight and want to lose twenty pounds because you feel you look bad. You decide to embark on an exercise program to recover the self-esteem that you base on physical attractiveness.

This approach is running from what you don't want. Ironically, what happens is that your success in the early stages of the process can undermine your continued commitment to the solution process. How? Let's say you lose five pounds in the first few weeks of the program. Then you feel less bad about your weight. There goes your motivation! You have lessened the level of self-contempt that caused you to embark on the program in the first place.

A Better Approach

A better approach is to look forward rather than backward. Instead of avoiding what you *don't* want (I don't want to be twenty pounds overweight), look forward to a "future-perfect" vision of what you do want (I want to be slim and vibrant).

If you look forward to when you are slim, attractive, more flexible, and can wear clothes that make you look and feel great, that vision will boost you to even greater motivation and excitement. You will progress toward your goal, rather than undermine it.

How could this process apply to your business, physical, or relationship goals? You might be surprised at the motivation you can generate to actually complete what you set out to do, instead of reinforcing doubt by giving up on those great intentions.

Reprogramming Your Lifetime Script

Re-scripting is not done easily—at first. You are reprogramming a lifetime script of conditioned reactions in favor of one based on a vision of your life goals. You are starting the vital process of moving toward what you actually want, rather than moving away from what you don't want. It is worth the effort.

Once you accomplish this re-scripting, you no longer limit your possibilities based on your past, and anything you really want in your future becomes possible to achieve. You can achieve your fullest potential.

The Circle of Wholeness

We all want to be whole, however we define it. In my practice and workshops, I find that people consistently want to deal with the issue of wholeness first. They experience losing that state of wholeness on a regular basis and want to learn how to recover it.

The Circle of Wholeness is a tool that will help you quickly and effectively determine where you currently are in different but interrelated domains, where you are relative to overall wholeness, and what your low and high areas are. The questions that accompany it will also show you how to raise both your lowest areas and your overall wholeness to catalyze greater happiness, fulfillment, and power.

You don't have to work on everything at once, only the lowest area. Doing so will raise all areas. Use this tool regularly and implement your corrections. You will notice a discernable difference in your personal power and joy. Don't use it, and you probably won't. I ask my clients to practice this exercise at least once a year—more often if they are feeling particularly imbalanced.

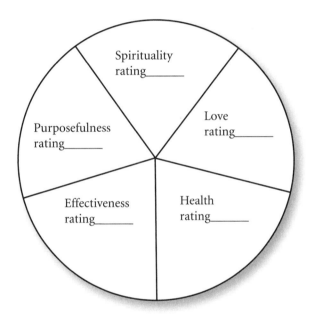

Complete it objectively and you will benefit from it! Rate each slice of the pie from 1 to 5, where 1 is horrible and 5 is excellent.

Here is what each slice of the pie means. Questions follow each definition.

Health—the emotional, mental, and physical vibrancy, energy, and balance with which you currently operate. How healthy and vital are you?

Love—your connection to and oneness with tangible entities, particularly people who are close to you. This category includes both how much you receive from those people or entities (such as nature, pets, or locations) and how much you give back to them. How much love do you experience?

Spirituality—your connection to that which is infinite and universal, that which was here before you were born and will be here after you are gone. How much spirituality do you practice in your thoughts, actions, and with other people?

Purposefulness—clarity of your individual purpose, your personal commitment to the highest gift you have to offer the world. How clear are you about your individual purpose, and how well are you fulfilling it?

Effectiveness—how masterfully you are growing and contributing toward an inspirational future in health, career, or relationships. How well are you practicing vision (leadership), process (management), and support (coaching) of yourself and others?

Add up your scores. Here is the rating system for the total:

21 to 25	A whole life
16 to 20	A partially whole life
10 to 15	A partially empty life
Less than 10	An empty life

Look at the area where you scored the lowest. Answer the following questions [4]:

1. What would be the impact on your total score if this area were a 5?

2. What would the impact be on the other areas of your pie if this lowest area were a 5?

---

[4] Go to www.integrativemasteryprograms.com/book/downloads.htm for a worksheet to help you complete this process.

3. What would you have to do to make it a 5?
4. Are you committed to doing that?

Action in one area starts the process and creates movement that will increase your score in that area. As your score moves up in that initial area, other scores will increase, as if by the domino effect. You will grow more fulfilled, conquer your limitations, and stop blaming others, the past, or life circumstances for what isn't working in your life. You will begin to look to the future for where you can make an impact, and stop holding yourself hostage to a past that you cannot change.

You will create true power and wholeness in your life.

After you complete this process for yourself, sincerely and honestly, help others you care for do the same. Have a conversation with them and share this Circle of Wholeness exercise.

What Is a Personal Life Vision?

Broadening your mind-set broadens your context for analyzing situations and will help you create a road map to your future from a larger identity than your ego.

How do you develop this alternative option of identity, intentionality, and mind-set? You create a Personal Life Vision (PLV). This is more than a personal credo or a sweet saying to be hung on the wall so others think well of you. It is a self-generated context for your best possible identity—who you are when you are not simply practicing ego-based behaviors.

You begin with a large list of values and reduce them to your top three core values: what means the most to you and what has the most impact on your world, the bigger world, and everyone in your world.

How would you like to be remembered at your funeral? What would you like people to say? That you were an expression of love? Of honor? Of excellent communication, selflessness, and generosity?

Once you identify your core values, you create a framework from which to practice them. For example:

> My personal life vision is a world where all people realize their fullest potential, a world of extraordinary relationships and extraordinary accomplishments, and a world where integrity and honorable actions are courageously pursued and commonly experienced.

This actually *is* my personal life vision. Let's break it down, line by line.

"My personal life vision is a world." I want this not just for myself, but for everybody else, even people who aren't born yet. I want to help create that world while I still can. Since my personal life vision is "a world," what I am striving for is big.

"A world where all people realize their fullest potential." Your life is a gift from God and what you do with it is your gift back to God. Therefore, your fullest potential is your unique gift—what wasn't here before you and what won't be here when you are gone. This is the best of yourself, the best way to use this life. My commitment is to help everyone realize his or her unique gift and develop a life centered on that gift. My commitment is to help others contribute to their friends, too.

"A world of extraordinary relationships . . ." We are here for a brief spark in eternity, at most a hundred years, often less. No man knows the hour of his own death, so we don't have time to play small. To me, extraordinary relationships keep us from being alone on the journey, help us connect with other people and feel grateful and generous toward them, and apologize when we make mistakes.

We can relate to people from a deep place and help them reach out to others. A life lived with full relationships is a full life; a life without close relationships is an empty life.

"...and extraordinary accomplishments." Since we are here for a short time, let's play big. I come from a family of risk-averse people. My dad worked for the government for forty years. When I finished high school, I thought I wanted a safe government job. I was scripted by his depression era psychology, but I awakened my entrepreneurial spirit and moved beyond that script.

I appreciate that we experience growth along with pain and setbacks as we take risks. These change us, and enlarge and accelerate the game. "Extraordinary accomplishments" means I play big, take risks and chances, and do things that test my edge of fear.

I recently motorcycled through Monument Valley. I was worried before I left because it is barren country. To control my fear, I prayed and meditated each morning to clear my mind. My companion's motorcycle broke down in the middle of Monument Valley, but we soon resolved the situation. Afterwards, my fear and anxiety evaporated.

We have to play big and take risks. I want that for everyone.

"A world where integrity and honorable actions are courageously pursued and commonly experienced." Integrity means that your words and actions match. It is the best of you. From thousands of hours of coaching successful people, I find their most common value is integrity. Integrity is something that most people can relate to and understand.

Honor is another common core value. To be honorable means that when you make a mistake, you make up for it and apologize. It doesn't embarrass you, it exalts you.

"Courageously pursued" means that it takes courage to practice values, to make a decision based on integrity and honor. "Commonly experienced" means that I promote my values in the world and encourage others to do the same.

I share my personal life vision with you because it is a powerful tool that I access at critical moments, especially when I lack motivation or am afraid or unsure. It is a larger mind-set from which I operate.

At this point, you may wonder how much of this is mere theory as opposed to something you can actually apply in your life. Let me give you some examples of how my clients and I use this powerful tool to create empowered solutions in a variety of areas.

- My marriage has been saved on at least three occasions by dealing with breakdowns using my Personal Life Vision (PLV) rather than my ego; my wife of thirty-one years uses her own PLV to join me in that approach.
- A young man's life was saved and then dramatically reversed toward extraordinary maturity and accomplishment after being suicidal over a broken relationship with his girlfriend.
- An executive who wanted her company to grow exponentially so it could be sold and fund her economic future did so. Over a five year period, she grew a modest business into an international company that sold for more than $30 million.
- A first-year college student used his PLV to overcome debilitating shyness and self-esteem issues, and he awakened positive and engaged relationships with college, his parents, and himself.
- A new regional manager from a Fortune 50 company took less than three years to raise his region from twelfth (of thirty-four) to number one in the nation.
- Several alcoholic executives overcame their addictions in favor of joyful sobriety and new leases on life.
- A client decided to lose weight and get healthy using his

PLV; he lost twenty percent of his body weight and reduced his belt size by six inches in six months.

- Countless clients who thought they had no spiritual beliefs developed strong spiritual outlooks and practices using their PLVs.
- Numerous companies and teams attribute their continued survival and success—sometimes even turnarounds—to the application of PLV; they began using successful and effective business strategies and tactics that were dramatically different from their previous approaches.
- Scores of people have replaced depression and despondency with joy and purpose by implementing their PLVs.
- I have coached an average of fifty executives and people in other positions each month—more than eight thousand hours of business and life coaching over nine years—using my PLV as my guide. Without it, I would have both failed and quit. With it, the past nine years have been one of the most joyful and fulfilling periods of my life (and, hopefully, the lives of my clients).

I could give you examples all day long, but you won't discover the life opening and empowering truth of what I am saying unless you create your own PLV and have the courage to practice your business and personal life as an expression of it. I ask that you become a living expression of your core values. If you do, I promise that you will transform your life into a dramatic, empowered manifestation of the best of your life potential. If you don't, I can promise that nothing will be very different for you than it is now.

From my PLV, I request that you take a chance: Believe me, and create and live your Personal Life Vision. Once you do, I would love to hear from you about how it has helped you fulfill your potential in business and life. As a dear friend and client recently wrote, "It amazes me how much my life vision contributes to my actions every day!"

Amaze yourself with how much power you have to transform your life or business if you are simply willing to command yourself to live as an expression of your own PLV. At the risk of sounding too ethereal, I literally consider the creation of a PLV a "whisper from your Soul" that will guide you to a bright, empowered, and fulfilled destiny if you let it.

If you look at the people we most revere, this is precisely what they did. They lived as expressions of their values, rather than allowing themselves to be limited by their egos, circumstances, or past scripts. Jesus, Buddha, Mother Theresa, Winston Churchill, Martin Luther King, anyone you can name. They were great because they personified greatness of values.

You can, too, if you are courageous enough to try it.

Determine Your Core Personal Values

1. Review the list of Core Values on page 29. Add any values that you think are missing, then copy the twenty values that mean the most to you.[5]

2. Choose the top ten of those twenty values and circle them.

3. Pick the top three of the ten you circled and write them on a clean piece of paper.

4. Write your precise definition of each of your top three values.

5. How would the world be different if these values were more present in your life and in those of everyone around you?

6. Are you willing to live your life as if these values were paramount?

---

[5] Go to www.integrativemasteryprograms.com/book/downloads.htm for a worksheet to help you complete this process.

7. If not, why not? If so, what will you change to bring
   yourself into alignment with these three values as you
   define them?

Core Values

This is a suggested list of values. Feel free to add anything you
don't find here, or change the wording to suit you.

___ Abundance	___ Faith	___ Organized
___ Accountability	___ Fame	___ Peace
___ Achievement	___ Family	___ Personal Development
___ Adventure	___ Fidelity	___ Personal Purpose
___ Ambition	___ Forgiving	___ Physical Challenge
___ Arts	___ Freedom	___ Pleasure
___ Authentic	___ Friendships	___ Power
___ Authority	___ Generous	___ Privacy
___ Awareness	___ Growth	___ Purity
___ Beauty	___ Harmony	___ Quality
___ Charity	___ Honesty	___ Recognition
___ Clean	___ Honor	___ Respect
___ Clarity	___ Humility	___ Religion
___ Community	___ Inspirational	___ Reputation
___ Compassion	___ Independence	___ Responsibility
___ Competence	___ Influence	___ Security
___ Competition	___ Inner harmony	___ Self-respect
___ Consciousness	___ Integrity	___ Serenity
___ Cooperation	___ Intelligence	___ Service
___ Courage	___ Involvement	___ Spirituality
___ Creativity	___ Joy	___ Stability
___ Decisiveness	___ Knowledge	___ Stewardship
___ Discipline	___ Leadership	___ Tolerance
___ Ecological awareness	___ Love	___ Tranquility
___ Effectiveness	___ Loyalty	___ Trust
___ Efficiency	___ Nature	___ Truth
___ Ethics	___ Natural	___ Wealth
___ Excellence	___ Open-minded	___ Wholeness
___ Excitement	___ Optimistic	___ Work
___ Expertise	___ Organic	

Create Your Personal Life Vision Statement

Review your list of Core Values and create a statement that represents your commitment for the future:
- Begin the statement, "My Personal Life Vision is a place/a world/a community . . ."
- Make the statement long enough to include your commitment, yet brief enough to memorize.
- Describe a future-perfect vision as though it has already become true.
- Specifically state your top three values to give substance, power, and meaning to your statement.
- Your statement is about you as well as others in the world, so be generous!

Future-Perfect: The Power of Your Mind

Each week we pass along a thousand ripples of influence and impact countless people. As long as we ignore the events the media tells us to be bothered by, life seems to be just fine. However, too often we find our moods shifting without being able to identify the source.

Make It or Break It

Join me in this visualization. I am on the 9th hole of a golf course facing a 3-foot putt. I find myself in one of two states of mind:

1. I run through the techniques of stance, grip, line, and ball position in my mind until I "think" I am ready to execute the putt. This approach is the mechanical, process oriented way to attempt the putt. Outcome? When I do it this way, I miss at least half of all the putts I attempt.

2. I approach the putt with a mind-set that assumes that the ball is definitely going in the cup. I even believe that the ball is *already* in the cup and all I have to do is allow what is already predetermined. Then, without too much setup or process, I simply putt the ball. Outcome? When I do it this way, I make about 90 percent of the putts.

Jack Nicklaus described the second way of putting during an interview. The writer asked him why he was such a good putter. Nicklaus, without hesitation, steadily looked the writer in the eye and said, "I've never missed a putt in my mind."

Beyond Golf

Something powerful is at work here that has greater implications for our lives than successful putts. It is as possible to establish a "future-perfect" mind-set for life as it is for putting. Use this great secret to create the results that you want.

A process oriented mind-set results from growing up in a conditioned response environment that rewards us for being good, and punishes us for being bad. Many of us are never introduced to the possibility of operating outside that mind-set, and we spend our lives mechanically and frenetically responding to circumstance, trying to receive rewards and avoid punishments.

Using even the best mechanical process to execute the putt limits our ability to create the result we want. However, when we entertain the thought that one of the possible results for the ball is to go into the cup, and that such a result is the perfect outcome, then we consciously choose to manifest that thought as if it had already happened in the future, as something beyond our rational/intellectual capacity.

The Key: View the event as though you are looking back on it, as though it already occurred.

Call it faith, the power of belief, intuition, or angels—but something else happens. When we open the possibility for something else to support us in creating the results we desire, our likelihood of achieving those results increases exponentially.

Your Desired Outcomes

Asking, "What do you want?" sounds simple on the surface. It is not so simple when viewed in a deeper way.

What determines your desired outcomes is the *source* of that desire. What you want ultimately depends on who you think you are. If your identity and the source of your desired outcomes are based only on comfort (pleasure, wealth, stimulation, euphoria, etc.), they come from the relatively small sphere of the ego. But if your identity and the source of your desired outcomes come from a place within you that encourages you to create a sense of deep, enlightened fulfillment and broader impact on the planet or your business, you will play a bigger game.

Ask yourself these questions:

1. What do I want? What is the greatest thing I could want, for the best reasons?
2. Who is asking for these outcomes? Do they benefit the most people, not just me?

Asking for what you want can be illustrated by two ways of praying. One way of praying is to negotiate or beg, hoping that whomever you pray to honors what you want. You muster up the faith that it will happen. The other way is to pray with the expectation that what you desire has already happened in the future. You keep your cynical part away from the possible disappointment if it doesn't happen just as you want it, and have faith that it will happen as it should.

Desired outcomes, while seemingly simple, are a critical monitor and measurement of who you are at present.

The Mask

As you consider mind-set, think about how you sometimes present a different image to the world. You don a mask that might not be the "face" you show all the time.

Imagine a world where everyone is born without a mask, yet grows one as they get older. This mask is invisible to the person wearing it. He is unaware of it except when other people make him aware of it through a look, a judgment, a comment, laughter, fear, or love. Those reactions may reflect approval or disapproval of the mask, and other people projecting their opinions on the mask don't always agree on how they see it.

What makes this mask unique is that the mask remains invisible even when the person wearing it looks in a mirror. It is only visible to others, and how others respond to it is how the person wearing it knows what it looks like.

The mask is also a pure reflection of the inner person wearing it. The mask instantly tells the world what that person believes, thinks, judges, and feels relative to the world and his place in it. It is an instant insight into his deepest self. Though he believes that nobody else knows him inside, in purest fact, everyone has seen him at that personal level and constantly responds to what they see. The mask allows people to see into others at the deepest level possible, but the wearer can never see his own mask.

A few people in this world have clear masks. They present themselves to the world through their masks as they know themselves to be at their very deepest level. But most of us have masks that are not that clear.

Here are some questions to consider about your own mask:

1. Imagine that when you look in the mirror, you can see a mask.
2. What is the mask that you present to the world?
3. Is this the façade you want people to see? Why or why not?
4. If this isn't a mask you want, what will you do about that?

Try It On

Put what you know on the shelf and practice being a learner, rather than a knower, when you are in an environment where you wish to learn or gather information. Try on what other people are saying, as though it might be true. You can throw it away if it does not work for you.

Allowing yourself to "try it on" from another's perspective is often an exponentially faster way to expand your knowledge than to simply do what you normally do, which is to compare all new information to the existing database of what you already know. That is the ego's process of reaffirming your sense of self. Unfortunately, it is a competing commitment to personal growth.

When you are in a learning mode and want to optimize your ability to really expand yourself, you should put on the perspective of the person you are with—the teacher, the mentor, the guru, the friend at lunch. From that perspective, try on what the teacher is saying as though it is true, without automatically shooting it down because it doesn't comply with what you already believe or know. You can always dismiss it afterwards, but you will often find that there is very little to object to and real growth can occur in a short period of time. It is one of the great secrets of exponential learning, rather than incremental learning.

It might even alter your mind-set.

Looking Forward

Now that your mind-set is clear, it is time to look at the problem or situation you have decided to tackle. We call this analysis Current Reality, and the next chapter describes how to examine it.

STEP 2
Current Reality Analysis

Each person comes into this world with a specific destiny. He has something to fulfill, some message has to be delivered, some work has to be completed. You are not here accidentally; you are here meaningfully. There is a purpose behind you. The whole intends to do something through you.

— Osho

The second critical step is an honest look at the current reality of your situation. This analysis has to be approached from a mind-set of personified values and principals, not ego.

If you skip the first step, mind-set, and simply jump into analyzing your current reality, then you will tend to go right into solutions and actions, which can limit you to the same models from which you currently operate, based on the same ego and success strategies you have used in the past. Can you see how this severely restricts your options?

Einstein said, "We cannot solve problems from the same mind-set that created them." An enlightened approach to your current reality analysis requires a mind-set of values and principals based on thinking that moves beyond personal scripts, comfort zones, ego, and success strategies to open a much wider realm of possibilities.

I am inviting you to examine your current reality objectively, without being overly judgmental about where you are right now. That said, your current reality does include everything leading up to where you are now. It could more accurately be called "past and current" reality.

How do you examine it without judgment? Look at a current situation in terms of what is working and what is not working, what is effective and what is not effective. This is different from looking at the situation as right or wrong. It allows a more objective analysis. From an external, objective perspective, you can see what is or isn't creating the results you want without coloring the situation with expectations, guilt, or old tapes.

Ethical discussions intrinsically limit your options because you become busy trying to incorporate your perception of morality or appropriateness to situations based on a moral or ethical code. This is dangerous ground because morality and ethics are usually formulated from an ego perspective. What is moral in some countries or cultures is considered immoral in others. We need some version of the "truth" that can be objective. Morality and ethics are typically subjective and, therefore, should be avoided when assessing a situation with the goal of pure understanding.

When we ask questions such as "What is working or not working?" or "What is effective or not effective?" we take into account all the variables at a subconscious, intuitive, and rational levels without the potential distortion provided by a more emotional, subjective, and personality influenced analysis.

An Example

Let's say that I always arrive at work late and I feel disorganized. If I say, "I am unprofessional," that statement is loaded with judgment. It is a declaration of what is wrong. "Unprofessional" is not what most people aspire to be.

This statement prevents me from finding creative, objective solutions. I start the entire analysis by undermining my own confidence and ability to face the issue successfully. What does that tell you about my chance of changing it? I will probably avoid doing anything about it.

On the other hand, if I approach the situation using the eight critical steps outlined in this book, I first say to myself, "I have a commitment to honor my life as a gift. I wish to use this gift as best I can. I am a steward of this life, and in my stewardship, I have to make every effort to take the best possible care of myself. I won't be perfect, but I will do the best I can."

When I approach it from that personification of my own honor and stewardship, I acknowledge my core values of integrity and self-care. Now I can look at my tardiness from outside myself and say, "I try to do too much. I make too many commitments. I stay up too late and can't get up on time. I don't allow enough time to accomplish tasks."

Do you see how these statements are more factual than opinions or judgments? I can look at what I'm doing or not doing and assess that honestly instead of with criticism.

I'm asking you to look at what isn't working from an objective standpoint, without judgment about how or why it happened—unless it is objectively relevant to solutions going forward.

Complaint or Commitment?

Robert Kegan and Lisa Laskow Lahey, two Harvard professors, wrote a book titled, *How the Way We Talk Can Change the Way We Work: Seven Languages for Transformation*. They analyzed complaints as one side of a coin and commitments as the other side. They saw that we can substitute the "language of personal responsibility" for the "language of blame." The book describes how leaders actually solict complaints from people in their organizations, rather than avoid them.

They point out to the complainers that implicit in their complaint is their commitment. For example, if my co-worker isn't working as hard as I am, I think she is overpaid and adds more burden on me. The alternative viewpoint is that I am committed to working hard for a fair paycheck and I expect my colleagues to do the same. I also believe that we should all be compensated in proportion to what we produce.

Do you see how people have something to work toward if we emphasize those commitments rather than the complaints?

How does this relate to your current reality analysis? If you analyze what is not working or what is not effective, instead of what is right or wrong, it is like a commitment instead of a complaint. If you say, "It's not effective right now for me to be late to meetings on a regular basis," you are revealing the commitment to be your optimal professional self.

As you complete your current reality analysis, look for areas where you can replace blame with commitment.

Let's get started.

My Current Reality Analysis

This stage often takes more time than the others because it demands a heartfelt, honest analysis of the situation and it begins to identify what we want to change. Please take some time to complete these exercises carefully.[7]

After you write down your initial thoughts, read through the rest of this chapter. As you think of additional data, add it. Then put it aside and come back to it in a few hours or the next day. Once

---

[7] Go to www.integrativemasteryprograms.com/book/downloads.htm for a worksheet to help you complete this process.

you enter the data into your subconscious mind, you will start to see other facets of the situation.

1. Describe the current situation so you are clear about what you are analyzing.
2. List everyone who has or could have anything to do with the situation.
3. Record what has already been done about the situation, if anything.
4. List what is working.
5. List what is not working.
6. List what has been effective.
7. List what has not been effective.
8. Write down your personal values that are emerging as important in this situation.
9. List who else you could ask to help you with this analysis to provide another point of view.
10. Send each person you listed a copy of these questions with a request to help you see the current situation from his or her point of view.

The Drunk in Vail

As you strive to see your current situation from every angle, read the following story, which shows the futility of creating life the "normal" way—trying to base happiness and fulfillment only on superficial achievement. I started to look at life differently, from my values rather than from petty outcomes, after encountering the drunk in Vail.

In 1995, I was wandering through a convention festival one evening in Vail, Colorado, watching the embarrassing antics of the drunken business folk away from home. I was alone and just making an appearance before returning to my room to prepare for the next morning's meetings.

41

As I walked past an outlying table, a friend hailed me. She sat with an elderly gentlemen who had six empty scotch glasses lined up like little crystal soldiers before their captain. He barely acknowledged me. Anne was clearly happy to see a friend. It wasn't clear whether the older fellow would last ten more minutes before collapsing into the empty little glass brigade lined up before him.

Anne asked me about my company's recent merger. I answered in detail, filling her in on the ups and downs of a newly merged company with four partners. She listened politely and nodded appropriately, each of us doing the same social dance that would have been entirely in place at court in France 300 years ago. It was a therapeutic conversation for me. I spewed out my concerns, fears, hopes, and problems while Anne absorbed the words like a mind-wandering queen with a boring diplomat.

After my overview, which I naturally felt was the perfect balance of insight and conclusion, the old fellow at the end of the table finally stirred.

"Young man, do you mind if I give you some advice?" he slurred.

I looked him up and down.

"Absolutely, I'd love it," I lied as convincingly as I could. *This ought to be good*, I thought to myself with the snide self-righteousness of an egoist who feels he knows it all, but must allow things to simply play out.

He looked at me with a discerning, if bleary, eye.

"I've listened to you explain to Anne about your company and I would like to give you a great secret to life," he explained. "But before I do, I should tell you that I have successfully used this secret to start, build up, and sell three different mortgage companies to Wall Street, including the one that your young friend here now works for."

He started looking a lot less drunk to me, and a lot more interesting.

He went on. "By using this secret, I've created great wealth and now have a house in Aspen, another in Naples, and more money than I can spend in this lifetime. However, I deeply regret not using this secret in my health or relationships, as I have two ex-wives I send a lot of alimony to, three kids who won't speak to me, and a stomach full of ulcers."

By now he had my rapt attention.

"What is it?" I asked.

He told me.

"Young man, I see you making the same basic mistake that most people do. We wake up in the morning and face a solid wall of problems. The problems are like little red lights embedded in the wall. We push on each light to put it out. All the while, we worry about all the other lights. After we put them out, some light up again. At day's end, we look at our wall of worry and although two-thirds of the lights are out, some still burn brightly. We collapse into bed and wake up the next morning with the wall all lit up again—solid lights."

He continued with the solution.

"The great secret to the wall of worry is to turn it into glass and see through it. Look through it into your imagined future three years forward and see exactly what you dream for your life. See it clearly. You don't have to know exactly how you're going to get there, but you do have to see it clearly and keep it in focus.

"If you leave the wall glass and continue to focus three years out, something magic happens. Little threads of solutions come back from that vision of the future and those threads put out the lights in the wall before you. I don't know who or what solves today's problems by creating tomorrow's dreams, or even how it happens, but I can sincerely promise you that this secret will change your life."

After thanking him, I returned to the condo to think about what I wanted for my future three years out, and what would inspire me to take action toward that future.

He was right. His secret changed my life. This is what happened:

- Within a few days, I created my three year dream: to find my great purpose in life by helping other people find theirs.

- I decided to sell my mortgage company and find a better venue for discovering and practicing my great purpose in life.

- I considered how I could make my company unique and develop a special expression of its value to differentiate it from other companies.

- Over the next several months, while still keeping my dream before me on a constant basis, a random article, a random conversation with an employee, and dozens of other influences ultimately helped me figure out how to sell my company. I would create an entirely new program for small and medium sized companies to offer their employees that would create huge revenues for our company and be a win/win for all of us.

- I approached my business partners with my idea and they cautiously let me proceed with it. The results? This program, which I called "Shared Dream," allowed my company to develop strategic alliances with 93 different companies and add 35,000 employees to our preferred customer program. Those new customers created $300 million dollars in new loans for our company in just three years and attracted a buyer for our company!

- My partners and I split the small profits when we sold the company. I found my current passion and started a new company of my own design, through which I can live my life's purpose to help other people find and live theirs!

It took me five years instead of three, but the Drunk in Vail's great secret literally changed my life, and it can change yours, as well, if you are simply willing to try it.

You will create your vision of the future in Step 3. For now, turn your wall of worry into glass and use your objective assessment of your current reality to start drawing to it the threads from your future. This will happen on its own as you continue to embody your values.

Are You Defensive?

As you consider your current reality for the situation or problem you want to work on using this book, do you notice yourself becoming defensive? Most people respond to a stressful situation in life defensively. Whether it is a disparaging remark from another person, a bad review at work, lack of work, or a wayward child, people are hardwired to respond defensively, even when such a response only makes the matter worse.

If you want to become more conscious about defensiveness, here is a new way to look at it and, if you choose to do so, move beyond it.

Defensiveness Opens Door #1

People go to Door #1 when under attack. They assess the situation from a "bunker" mentality by asking themselves if there is an immediate threat to their image, well-being, or survival. If not, they play the "what if" game to see where the situation might go. They assess each negative possibility to determine if it threatens their image, well-being, or survival.

Once the adverse situation is perceived to be a threat—which it almost always is—people typically respond in one of two ways:
- Secretly Aggressive: They don't react outwardly; instead, they stockpile resentment, fear, and negative feelings until they explode at some point in the future.

45

- Openly Aggressive: They immediately attack the person they imagine is responsible for the situation.

Door #1 responses eventually lead to Door #2. When someone gets tired of the mental fight to be right, he finally throws in the towel and implements Door #2.

Door #2 Abandons the Relationship

At Door #2, the person under attack gives up the mental battle and decides to abandon the relationship. He often demonizes the person or situation he thinks caused the situation. The relationship may move from temporary breakdown to permanent breakdown.

Most people live their entire lives oscillating between Door #1 and Door #2. The result is a life of frustrated misunderstanding, victim mentality, and constant attempts to find happiness in a new company, career, spouse, or location.

Fortunately, the third door offers a way out. When you decide to move from the disempowered state of hoping that things will get better (by giving others the power to fix the situation), to the empowered state of commitment to action (where you accept accountability for results), then Door #3 opens.

Door #3 Is the Conscious Response

Door #3 is the conscious response to adversity using three basic components:

1. Ruthless compassion in which you stick to the facts and avoid an inflammatory story as much as possible.
2. Commitment to effectiveness, rather than perceived "rightness."
3. Bold confrontations resulting in breakthrough solutions to the barriers creating adversity.

With Door #3 you "pierce the heart of the dragon," with a clarifying dialogue that embraces these three components.

When you discuss the adverse situation with ruthless compassion, you achieve total objectivity beyond the protection of feelings or perceptions of "rightness." This allows true commitment to the most effective response, rather than to a politically correct or popular response based on how you look to yourself or others.

This occurs by directly confronting the person or situation in a way that validates rather than diminishes everyone and keeps defensiveness at bay. This technique allows people to operate from a high state of empowered action, not the state of self-protection that is characteristic of Door #1.

Review your Current Reality Analysis, examining it with this tool in mind. Is it based on defensiveness or abandonment of the situation? Revise it to include analysis from Door #3.

Do You Have Faith?

The root of faith is the courage to believe in something that is not guaranteed. Courage involves taking a risk. Faith is bold, brave, and critical to happiness. Faith is the antidote to doubt.

You need to have faith at all levels:

- Faith in yourself and others, rather than doubt and cynicism
- Faith in your Source,[8] rather than your temporary mortality
- Faith in your business when you have tough days
- Faith in your ability to overcome problems when no solutions are apparent

How is Enlightened Faith different from normal faith?

---

[8] Throughout this book we occasionally refer to Divinity, God, Source, the Universe, the Tao, as "your Source." Please substitute any other word that represents this concept best to you.

Normal faith is ego based. It operates in areas where it is easy for us to have faith. I may say, "I have faith in General Motors because they have been around forever and I know they'll never go away." When they enter bankruptcy, my world shifts. It was outside my paradigm to think they would ever have a problem.

Once my world shifts, I may see that I have been operating from blind faith. And if that happens, I have opened myself to the opportunity of achieving an Enlightened Faith level, which is beyond what we consider even possible. It is larger in scope and more universal in implication than blind faith.

Unenlightened faith resides mostly inside my mind; Enlightened Faith is more like the mind of Source or the mind of God. Unenlightened faith is faith from the ego; Enlightened Faith is faith from the Soul. It is from our largest, deepest self.

In addition to the courage that faith intrinsically requires, Enlightened Faith also takes vision and heart. With Enlightened Faith, virtually everything is possible.

Review your Current Reality Analysis and look for instances of unenlightened faith in what is not working, and instances of Enlightened Faith in what is working. Enjoy your successes.

Are You Too Comfortable?

Jim is an Ironman.[9] He inspires me because he has taken sixth place for his age group in the Super Bowl of Ironman competitions, the annual event in Hawaii. He is in the best physical condition of anyone over fifty that I have ever known.

Jim accomplishes these amazing feats by practicing "commitment" instead of "comfort." He exercised five hours a day for many years to achieve this level of mastery. Despite discomfort, his burning

---

[9] An Ironman competition requires a 2.4 mile swim, followed by a 112 mile bike ride, followed by running a full 26.2 mile marathon.

commitment toward his vision of himself as a champion athlete kept him moving toward that goal.

Sue is another example. She is a multi-gold medal champion in bicycle racing. She also followed her commitments rather than succumbing to the comfort of a sedentary lifestyle.

Gandhi did it with India. Mother Theresa did it with the poor in Calcutta.

On the other hand, my mother chose to be comfortable. She sat down in a lounge chair around age fifty and began watching soap operas. She thought it might be even more fun and comfortable with a little cocktail. She spent her last twenty-five years in that chair, in a subtly increasing state of depression, poor physical health, and self-questioning dialogue about the meaninglessness of her life. She started to doubt that her earlier accomplishments had ever occurred and died in a dispirited and lonely state.

Like most people, you probably operate from both comfort and commitment. Look at your great accomplishments and see if you sacrificed comfort to operate from inspired commitment. Perhaps you can also remember a time when you were miserable and didn't know how to get out of that place. Maybe the cause was the subtle stagnancy and growth inhibiting nature of comfort.

Many clients have said that hearing me declare that comfort is the enemy was the greatest single coaching statement I had ever shared in support of their lives. Although it accounts for countless breakthroughs, we often don't look at why it works so well.

What is your comfort zone? Where do you go, mentally or physically, to retreat from your daily life? Do you go there to eliminate discomfort stress and pain? Jot down some thoughts.

How does this become self-limiting? When does it get in the way of accomplishing what you really want in life?

To identify when to choose to operate from commitment rather than comfort, look at your state of mind. If you are unhappy, stressed, depressed, empty, discouraged, or pessimistic, you may need to recommit to an inspired future. We naturally blame the circumstances of our lives. ("I'm too busy." "I have no time for myself." "Nobody appreciates me.") By blaming and reacting to circumstances, you preclude your ability to change those states of mind. You give control to the circumstances and can only react to them.

To take back your power, you need to create an inspirational future. When you envision a future so big that you desire it more than the comfort that is currently your priority, you no longer limit your actions to your comfort scripts. Becoming aware of this process and consciously practicing a committed approach to life creates a desired, inspiring future. It takes persistence, practice, patience, and support. Commitment is about growth and empowerment. It lays the foundation of personal growth.

Comfort is about stagnancy and past scripts. It is our enemy, cloaked as a friend.

How has your state of mind helped create the situation you want to change? Return to your Current Reality Analysis and identify or add where comfort has taken priority over commitment. What can you change to support your new state of mind?

What Is Your Work Style?

Here is one final story that will let you take another view of your Current Reality Analysis before you move to the next step, Future Outcome.

Susie likes to work hard and get things done. Everyone looks to her when they need to make progress on a task force, make the copier work, or make sure that jobs are moving forward. She is the go-to person to solve everyone's problems. Susie is the company's "Gardener."

Tom is a visionary leader. He sees the big picture and loves to talk about big ideas. He can easily see things from an overview and articulate convincingly and passionately what the possibilities are in virtually any situation. He inspires others into action. Tom is the company's "Rocket Man."

Susie would tell you that she does all the work and is tired all the time. She doesn't believe that anyone else can do any job as well as she does, and she simultaneously resents how little time she has to spend with her family. She would mention that her health has been starting to suffer.

Tom would say that his life is great because he sees opportunity everywhere. However, he might mention that his desk is disorganized, he has too many half started projects, and he hates being drawn into everyone's petty problems. In fact, he would say that he becomes angry when he has to stop and solve these problems because they interrupt his solving larger issues using his vision and influence. He notices that he changes jobs often, thinking the "grass always seems greener" in other places. In truth, although he appears happy, he's drinking a little too much and isn't very satisfied.

Let's look more closely at "The Rocket Man" and "The Gardener."

The Rocket Man flies at 30,000 feet and can see great distances. Below him, he sees an ocean to the left, a forest to the right, and farmland directly beneath him. He sees opportunity in all of them. However, while he sees opportunity everywhere—which we call vision—he often lacks the ability to land on the ground and pick up a shovel to do any "real work." He is motivated by the inspiration of his vision. Digging in the dirt with a shovel seems beneath him, too hard physically, and relatively boring.

The Gardener, on the other hand, has her feet firmly planted on the ground. She readily picks up a shovel and digs feverishly in the dirt. She derives great satisfaction from weeding her garden, planting seeds, watering them, killing bugs, and harvesting crops.

She works long and hard, but sometimes runs out of energy. She often feels martyred by "doing all the work." She also feels under-appreciated by others, especially the Rocket Man.

Each role is self-limiting. Each is inadequate, by itself, to create true effectiveness. True effectiveness comes from seeing opportunity and envisioning possibilities from on high (the domain of the Rocket Man), merged with purposeful action in the dirt of actual work toward the goals (the domain of the Gardener).

True effectiveness is personal mastery. Personal mastery is the practice of effectively marrying vision with action.

Return to your Current Reality Analysis. Are you the Rocket Man or the Gardener? How has one of those attitudes informed your present situation?

What Are Your Strengths and Weaknesses?

This tool requires you to be honest and objective about your strengths and weaknesses, as if you were looking at someone other than yourself. This analysis lets you craft a pathway forward to overcome your weaknesses and amplify your strengths.

Some things are genetic. Some body types prevent people from having careers as professional basketball players (although exceptions to that exist as well), but you can still be far more healthy or dynamic than you have allowed yourself to be in the past.

Remember Jim, the Ironman? What drives him is far beyond pure genetic gifts. Yes, he has them, and he trained hard for thirty years until it became an inner quest. He is now someone who goes out and runs twenty miles or bikes a hundred miles on a Saturday. His discipline has optimized his strength. It has given him the opportunity to be a world-class athlete in an endeavor that few human beings have even tried.

Can you imagine how he is in other areas when he has a tough day?

Now look back over your life and answer these questions:

1. Identify your greatest strengths and the impact they have had on your life.

2. Pinpoint your greatest weaknesses and the impact they have had on your life.

3. List some ways you could amplify your strengths going forward to have more of those positive impacts.

4. List some ways you could consciously recognize your weaknesses in the moment and operate in new ways so they don't limit you or your outcome.

Looking Forward

Keep your strengths and weaknesses in mind as you begin to build your desired future outcome in Step 3.

Inspired Future Outcome

Don't be afraid of Death, be afraid of the unlived life. Birth is not one act, it is a process. The aim of life is to be fully born though its tragedy is that most of us die before we are thus born. To live is to be born every minute. Death occurs when birth stops.

— Erich Fromm

Put aside your Current Reality Analysis for a moment to envision your big dream. Creating your Inspired Future Outcome is the third critical step.

Consider your problem or situation. What would make it perfect? Think generously, creatively, and limitlessly about all possible desired outcomes. This type of thinking is challenging because it requires looking at the underpinnings of your assumptions.

Later in this chapter you will be invited to think about 1000 outcomes! The bigger your outcome, the more momentum you will create. You move from your current reality to your inspirational outcome when the future outcome is bigger than the current reality. The gravitational pull this generates is called creative tension, which you will learn about in the next section.

To ensure your future outcome is as large as possible, complete the exercises in this chapter.

Creative Tension

Creative tension is a critical concept that creates the foundation for integrated mastery. It is something we will return to again and again. As you consider your Current Reality Analysis, creative tension is a way to move beyond the paralysis of your current perspective.

All artists start with a blank canvas, which is their current reality. To turn that canvas, or piece of paper, or block of marble into a work of art, they have to do certain things to it. This process can be applied to all areas of life and is called creative tension.

From the current reality, the artist creates a vision of what he wants in the future that is bigger than his current reality. This creates tension between where he is and where he wants to be with that finished piece of art. Since tension naturally seeks resolution, pressure is created.

Pressure naturally seeks resolution and the resolution of this pressure is for the current reality to move toward the artist's vision of the finished work. You can apply the same process in your job, relationships, or health.

Imagine two iron balls on an icy lake connected by a gigantic bungee cord. If current reality is one iron ball and the vision of the future is the other, the bigger iron ball will pull the opposite one to it. If your fear and despondency of your current situation is bigger than your vision of the future, then your vision of the future will collapse into your current reality.

If Leonardo Da Vinci had thought about how blank the canvas was and how hard it would be to turn it into the Mona Lisa, he might never have started, or he might have started and quickly become discouraged. However, since his vision of the finished project was clear, he was able to generate a masterpiece.

Values and passion matter because they give you the courage to create large visions that are bigger than your fears. Creative tension gives you the awareness to look objectively at current reality and the courage, boldness, scope of vision, passion, and inspiration to create a much bigger vision of the future than you are experiencing in the current reality. In addition, it requires you to keep both in mind at the same time.

Along the way some dynamics occur. You may be doubtful, thinking, *Who am I to do this?* Answer these doubts with thinking that goes like this: *I may be nobody, but my vision is so great that it will be worth taking action toward. With faith, and by doing whatever it takes, I will succeed. Even if I'm not perfect, my resolve is unconditional and I will start toward it and keep going until I reach it.*

When you operate from your values, you gain access to the courage to create a large vision without letting doubt get in your way. Doubt is the source of suffering and faith is the antidote.

The important thing is not what the vision is, but what the vision does. Many people throughout history set out to do one thing and ended up doing something else that mattered far more. Many medical discoveries, such as penicillin, happened as a result of what the vision *did* rather than what the vision *was*. You, too, can create these results by using the tools in this chapter. You invite Providence to be your partner when you have the vision, values, and resolve to generate and act from the power of creative tension.

Starting with your Current Reality Analysis, what "home run" outcome or inspirational future would dramatically improve or evolve an area of your life?

How Do You Want to Be Perceived?

As you create your vision, it is important to see yourself in it. By knowing who you are, or who you want to be, you set yourself up to be able to fulfill the vision. One of the most common challenges in creating a worthy vision is to determine your great life purpose, the one thing that will fulfill your life and career. I call this "achieving the critical mass of your life's value proposition." Let's look at each of those terms:

Critical mass occurs when something is self-perpetuating or self-propelling without the catalytic requirement of an outside agency. In other words, the thing becomes self-fulfilling. A nuclear reaction, for example, achieves critical mass when it creates further reaction from within itself, rather than through the scientist's intervention from the outside.

Value proposition is the value you offer in exchange for some value you get back. It is important to achieve critical mass of your value proposition at work whereby your value becomes self-evident to those it serves. When this state is reached, those served by your value naturally respond and compensate you in return.

We all offer value propositions every day to our employers, partners, children, community, and nation. Unfortunately, most of us are unaware of what our personal value proposition is, and we live our lives thinking it is what we have to do for others to get what we want in return (such as a paycheck), rather than a reflection of something far more significant (an expression of our values in action).

This shift of perspective on your value proposition begins the process of fully living and allows your value proposition to become a source of life fulfillment, not merely a different way to present your intentions to others.

My father, for example, worked for the federal government for forty years without enjoying it. He did it to make money that he hoped would allow his family some fulfillment. As an old man, he wondered who he really had been all those years, how much it mattered that he had performed those duties, and what he could have been had he approached life from a more inspired, empowered, and risk tolerant mind-set.

The five steps to achieving the critical mass of your value proposition are:

1. Define your value proposition in light of the problem or situation you are working on.
2. Define who your value proposition serves within that problem or situation.
3. Grow awareness of your value proposition to those it serves.
4. Let others experience your value proposition authentically by providing it with the pure intention and actions of your values personified.
5. Achieve critical mass by providing and refining what you give through bold, consistent integrity.

Let's look at each step in detail.

Step 1: Define Your Value Proposition

Most of us are in one of these phases:
- The Young Child Phase
- The Adolescent Phase
- The Adult Phase

Phase 1: Young Child—Disempowered Phase

In this least empowered phase, we are at an unfulfilled level of empowerment and purpose, based in control by others. This phase can be characterized as: "Mom thinks I am a good kid."

Until puberty, we derive our identity from our parents or family structure. Our identity is closely associated with the value we believe we offer to others, so we think that our value is limited to what others want us to do: get good grades, pick up our room, and be respectful. We have little independent value beyond fulfilling what others expect of us. In return, we receive love, support, and acceptance.

Phase 2: Adolescent—Semi-Empowered Phase

In this modestly empowered phase, we are at an unfulfilling level of empowerment and purpose, based on ego, image building, and self-conscious actions. It could be characterized as: "My value proposition is what I do for others in exchange for money, validation, or perceived power."

Between puberty and adulthood, we begin to develop an independent identity based on a broader context of how others see us and who we believe ourselves to be, based on our interests, image, and activities. We become conscious of our peers and want them to perceive us in a positive way, for example, as smart, pretty, kind, or hardworking. We validate ourselves as an ego and gain the ability to build a more independent identity than how our parents see us. Among other impacts, it makes separation from our parents tolerable and even desirable.

Since identity is closely associated with value, in Phases 1 and 2 we become trained to think that our value lies in what we do. We work at the ice cream store at sixteen, slinging ice cream for minimum wage. Later we go to college or study a chosen discipline to become trained, certified doers of some activity in exchange for compensation.

As a result, if we become lawyers, for example, we spend the rest of our working lives with the value proposition of providing legal advice to others in exchange for money, power, and prestige. Most people never consider going beyond this phase of identity and value.

Phase 3: Adult—Empowered Phase

With the final evolution to the fully empowered phase, we finally realize a fulfilling level of empowerment and purpose based in our personified values.

People who reach this level have clarified their core values and are willing to personify them in lieu of the limiting actions of comfort-based egocentrism. Once you know what values you will stand for and you live life as an expression of those values, you increasingly become a living manifestation of them.

Over time, one's values generate more power and impact and exponentially contribute to the well-being of others. At this level, a person's identity becomes the driving force over his actions, and what he can actually accomplish with his actions becomes dramatically more effective and fulfilling for all concerned. In addition, these people tend to bring out this same level of values based identity in others, creating great families, companies, communities, and countries.

Gandhi, Martin Luther King, Mother Theresa, and Winston Churchill, all operated at this level. Both you and I could operate in this way, too.

The step of defining your identity and value proposition is critical because operating at the Adult Phase sets up the scope and success of the four steps that follow. Defining yourself as less than this sets up mediocre and disappointing results.

Step 2: Identify Who Your Value Proposition Serves

The next step in life empowerment is to identify who needs and is served by your value proposition. The higher your phase of identity, the more people are served by it.

- A Phase 1 person may mow the lawn, be a good student, or work at an ice cream store, and accordingly serve people who want a groomed lawn, good students, or good employees. The compensation from those served may be: limited to a few dollars for a mowing; proud, loving parents; or a minimum wage paycheck.

61

- A Phase 2 person serves a specific function of business or service, helping organizations accomplish profitability or their mission. He may become a mere cog in the machine, fulfilling the dreams of others in exchange for a paycheck. Most of us live here, often sacrificing personal fulfillment.
- A Phase 3 person lives his life as an expression of his committed values, experiencing integrated empowerment in his work, and deriving a fulfilled life from serving others. Mystically, the Source seems to somehow encourage and actively support people at this level.

Step 3: Market Your Value Proposition

After identifying who is served by the value in your value proposition, you have to make them aware of it. The lawn mowing boy hands out fliers and the lawyer puts an ad in the telephone book. The Phase 3 person, however, needs this marketing level only initially, for once he reaches Step 4, he achieves critical mass and requires little or no marketing.

Step 4: Let Others Experience Your Value Proposition

Now that people know you exist and how your value proposition may serve them, they may be willing to engage you. Once they do, what they experience will determine whether they:
- don't receive what you promised and never use you again
- receive what you promised and do use you again
- were so impressed with the experience of value you provided that they actively refer you to others

When you serve others from the last position, you become recognized for core values such as love, commitment, integrity, or honesty and help people realize the importance of values based living. You invite them to a more empowered and noble place within themselves from which they can more consciously manifest their own values.

Over time, the people you impact want others to experience what they experienced, and refer new people to you. As this happens, you don't need to market yourself as much because people seek you out. Then you can use your marketing time to deepen and grow your value proposition even more, which takes you to Step 5.

Step 5: Step Into Fulfillment

Achieving critical mass of your value proposition occurs when you spend less time marketing (Step 3) and more time serving others in a meaningful way (Step 4). It is the level where work and life are balanced and fulfilling.

Here, your balance of life does not compete with your work, but is simply an extension of it. People throughout history have accomplished this, and we hold them in the highest regard. For example, Gandhi created an independent India and was a historically great leader. A million people went to his funeral because he had personified purposefulness, truth, peace, and humility, and he had invited his followers to practice the same values.

To evaluate how you are perceived, answer the following questions:

1. What situation are you working on?
2. What phase do you tend to live from in this situation? 1, 2, 3?
3. If you wrote down Phase 1 or 2, what could you do to move to Phase 3 by living more consistently from your values?
4. Who does your value proposition serve?
5. How will you market your value proposition?
6. How big will you ultimately manifest your value proposition?

7. In what ways will you balance your life once you achieve critical mass with your value proposition?

Visions vs. Dreams

Now that you see who and how you are, you can create your bigger vision around that perspective of yourself. People talk of visions and dreams interchangeably, according to how future oriented their mind-set is. People stuck in the past usually evoke thoughts and discussions based on memories, history, and past experiences. People who speak of their visions or dreams are generally less concerned with the past, other than how it impacts their future.

Both visions and dreams are critical components in creating a future and the absence of both generally precludes the ability to create a defined future. Visions differ from dreams in both scope and power.

Dreams primarily occur during unfocused fantasies or sleep. When we are unconscious, as in sleep, we are disempowered. Daydreams are similarly ineffective for creating realized futures because they lack the compelling individual commitment that manifests tangible reality.

Visions, on the other hand, are created or experienced consciously. They are created purposefully. They generally involve benefit to a group of people or a company and are, therefore, not simply for the sole benefit of their creator. Often they create intense commitment from people working together.

In short, visions are empowering and dreams are not. Visions are more likely to materialize through focused commitment from the people embracing them, while dreams rarely escape from their fantasy world.

Futures can only be consistently manifested when they start as visions, rather than dreams.

Are you more of a dreamer or a visionary?

If you could envision anything in the world right now that would dramatically improve your life or the lives of others, what would it be?

What would it take for you to commit to actually making that vision a reality?

The Wizard of Oz

Sometimes we have trouble creating our visions because we are hung up on beliefs or illusions that are not even true. Let's look at illusions and how we hide behind them until we are exposed.

One of our most compelling stories is about Dorothy visiting the Wizard of Oz in the 1939 movie starring Judy Garland. It is a wonderful metaphor for how we hide our actual identities and project what we think others want to see. We may do this from insecurity or manipulation, amplified ego, or hopeful projection of our ideal selves, but it often bespeaks a fear of being found out, as the Wizard of Oz experienced.

Most of us avoid, at all costs, being perceived as inferior or unworthy of the favor, trust, or love of others. If we project a version of ourselves designed for the audience's consumption rather than one that accurately reflects who we really are, how real is our worth to the audience? What did Dorothy and her friends have to do to get through to the Wizard?

Expose him.

After he was exposed, what did the Wizard do? He stopped over-promising and under-delivering. He stopped promising what he knew they wanted to hear. He began to be truthful with the challenges and solutions for the Lion, Tin Man, Scarecrow, and Dorothy. By allowing himself to be just a man, with all of his flaws, they could finally regard him as a real source of information.

After the Wizard's balloon took off without her, even Dorothy realized that her solution had been available to her all along. In the end, she only needed the Wizard to help her see the obvious solution.

How can you apply this to your life? The next time you are in a meeting, reviewing an employee, talking to a customer, or playing with your children, challenge yourself by posing this question internally: *Who am I being right now?* Are you the Wizard behind the curtain, projecting an image that isn't really you? Are you kidding anyone with your projection, or do they know the Wizard is behind the curtain?

How much more effective and fulfilling would your life be if you had the courage to expose your actual identity and create the possibility of real trust and connection to others?

Experiment: 1000 Futures

Now that you are ready to "be real," imagine that you have 1000 futures before you, ranked from 1 to 1000 (1 being the absolute worst, 1000 being absolutely fabulous).

1	250	500	750	1000
Worst	Fairly bad	Neutral	Fairly good	Best

Above 500, imagine increasing states of exhilarated perfection, and 999 as heaven—the ultimate outcome. All of the thousand future outcomes are ripe with implications and assumptions in terms of possibilities and capacities, both good and bad. Don't limit yourself.

For example, look at the situation you described in the Current Reality Analysis you created in Step 2. On the above scale from 1-1000, where would you rate it? _____ Now project forward from your present situation to the most likely number equivalent you foresee for it in the future. What number is that? _____

How many more numbers are there from your projected number to 1000?

1000

— ____ Your projected number

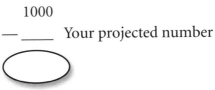

This number represents how many possible futures are available to you that are better than the one you are currently awaiting!

Now answer the following questions:

1. Using either your original number or your projected one, describe what #987 would look like compared to either number. Dream freely, as if you can have whatever you want, regardless of the path you are currently on.

2. Thinking creatively and in bold, new ways, what would you have to change or do to construct an effective pathway to the #987 you just described?

3. What will you do to put your process into action?

Spectrum of Opportunity

The Spectrum of Opportunity is a way to explore your 1000 futures.

I developed this tool years ago, after the only time I was fired from a job. I had built up a company with some partners and we sold it to a group of wealthy Tennessee bankers. A year or two into this experiment, they fired several company leaders, including me. Later, I sat in the parking lot wondering what had just happened, taking it personally, and sifting through the reasons why it had happened. I concluded that my flaws had finally become as apparent to my bosses as they were to me.

After some wonderful coaching from my wife to view it as an opportunity rather than a tragedy, I developed The Spectrum of Opportunity. First, I made a list of thirty people in my network to talk to. Because I cared about these friends and business associates, I assumed they reciprocated my feelings. I set up daily lunches, breakfasts, coffees, and meetings in their offices over the course of a month.

I shared with each my Spectrum of Opportunity possibilities. I talked about different jobs or pursuits I was considering. I gave each a rating from 0 (hell) to 1000 (heaven):

- Shoe salesman – 88
- Truck driver – 192
- Starting a mortgage company – 592
- Executive for another mortgage company – 620
- Public speaker – 720
- Writing a book – 850

At each meeting I asked, "What do you see that I don't see about these and do you have any that I should add to this list?"

They gave me suggestions and I added each with a rating.

This exercise did several things:

- It gave me clarity about some of the 1000 futures before me, weighted by the ratings.
- It helped me network with people and let them know I was available.
- It helped me tap into their creative thoughts about what I could do.
- It gave them the opportunity to contribute to my search and support me.
- It gave me confidence, got me out of the house, and kept me from professional depression and the urge to lock myself away in the basement.

On the thirtieth day, I met with a longtime friend who had a perfect career idea for me. After some encouragement and investigation, I chose to pursue it in earnest, leading to a series of events that I believe fulfilled the Universe's plan for me and culminated in my current profession, which I consider to be the fulfillment of my professional and personal life.

Invite the support of the Universe by taking some steps on your own to consider the spectrum of opportunities before you. Remember that God helps those who help themselves. Invite the input of other people to help you discover what doors to open.

This is a particularly valuable tool for anyone who is in a job transition or considering a new job role.

Use your journal or download the worksheet from our website, www.integrativemasteryprograms.com/book/downloads.htm

1. What is the situation facing you now that has you feeling stuck, stagnant, or uncertain?
2. Make a list of every possible solution, no matter how strange or silly it seems. Assign a number between 0 and 1000 that represents how appealing it is to you. Fill every box with a potential solution.
3. List twenty-five people you could ask for input about your list.
4. Set up meetings with each of these people. Attend the meetings and I promise that evolution will come from this process.

Looking Forward

Now that your vision is clear, it's time to execute it. The next step is creating the road map that will give you a clear plan to follow.

The Road Map

Whatever you can do or dream you can, begin with boldness. Boldness has genius, power, and magic in it. Until one is committed, there is hesitancy, a chance to draw back, always ineffectiveness. The moment one definitely commits oneself, then Providence moves too. All sorts of things occur to help one that would never otherwise have occurred.

— Goethe

The fourth of the eight critical steps is moving from your current reality to your desired and inspired future while following your vision and maintaining the mind-set shaped by your values. You accomplish this by creating a road map of resolute action.

This chapter will help you create your road map. You will determine actions to take and identify milestones of progress to encourage your continuous commitment to the process. Because this project is more like a marathon than a sprint, it is important to measure your progress so you don't grow impatient or discouraged. Your milestones and actions will be specific, measurable, and have time frames. You will also identify who can help you execute the action steps.

This step often takes more time than the other steps, so please devote as much time as you need to complete the process with sincerity, resolve, and faith in yourself.

You will build your actual road map at the end of this chapter with the Echo of Empowerment exercise. Before you get there, however, it is important for you to understand some preliminary concepts that will help you be more open to possibilities when you get there.

The Road in Arizona

Imagine that one day you magically find yourself in a car going seventy-five miles per hour down one of those vast highways in Arizona. Curiously, you are alone in the car, yet you are somehow tied over the front seat facing backwards. You are looking straight out the rear window and your feet are hooked into the steering wheel to guide the car. You decide on corrective actions by looking at the road behind you. The car is on cruise control, so your speed is steady.

You find that you are comfortable. The seat seems to support you in such a way that moving only causes discomfort, and the road is straight enough that you don't really have to steer much to continue in a straight line. After all, as long as the road you leave behind is straight, can't you presume the road ahead will remain so?

Suddenly, you notice the edge of the pavement nearing the left side of the car, so you have to steer into a curve. You adjust the steering enough to stay in your lane on the road and not over steer into oncoming traffic, which you see whizzing past you out your back window.

With a growing sense of dread, you realize that a really curvy road lies ahead. There may even be switchbacks. It will be impossible to anticipate the changes in direction. You will go off the road if you don't do something.

You realize that the road you are leaving behind in no way indicates the road ahead. What was straight and easy to drive in the past may be curvy and dangerous in the future. First you feel fear, then panic, and then you cry out for help from anyone who may be listening.

Why is this happening? What have you done to deserve the sure fate that awaits you as your car swerves through curve after curve, barely staying on the pavement? Surely there is a great injustice at work here! You did nothing to deserve such a fate. You have driven your car as well as anyone could while looking out the back window, haven't you? Who could do better?

Now imagine you make one simple change: You remember that you don't have to look out the back window. You work yourself free of the straps holding you in place and turn around to sit in the driver's seat, facing forward and driving with your hands on the wheel while looking out the front windshield.

The road now seems clear, safe, and even enjoyable. You see curves coming and easily negotiate them. You see mountains, valleys, other cars coming at you, and all the road configurations coming your way. None frighten you anymore. You are really driving now!

Looking up, you notice the rearview mirror and watch the road behind you recede into the distance. You realize that you can still see where you have been, and what you have learned from your travels, but you are no longer controlled by your past. You have clarity and control driving forward, along with the ability to see behind you, all at the same time.

You notice that you are more relaxed and confident because driving is so much easier this way. You have time to drive masterfully, yet still look around and enjoy the scenery. Looking down, you notice two more things that excite you. First, you can control the speed with the gas pedal and brakes. Your car's speed is now within your power. Second, you notice the GPS built into the dashboard. This marvel of technology helps you direct your car to any destination, merely by asking.

How does this parallel your life? Is this a metaphor for your existence? It is a guideline for how you can "drive" your life. You can look at past actions, tendencies, trends, histories, and thoughts and doom yourself to acting as though they control where you go—like driving while looking out your back window.

Or you can turn around, look at road ahead, and determine your direction, speed, and path to where you want to go—like looking out the front window. You can even use the GPS to track your path to a distant destination you envision in your mind's eye. All it takes is the recognition that you may be driving your future from the point of view of your past, the commitment to change your view from backward to forward, and the willingness to go through temporary discomfort while changing your viewpoint.

You can let your vision turn you forward to your future, instead of using your past to avoid what you don't want and hoping that your future works out.

How would your life be different if you navigated toward your future rather than away from your past? Do you have the courage and commitment to turn around and start driving forward? What will you have to change to do this?

Promise Based Management

As you create your road map, you require management. While leadership is about creating a vision of the future unlimited by the past, management is about the tactical, tangible actions that move a process forward. The difference between "behavioral management" and "promise based management" is critical.

Everyone needs behavioral management to control outcomes. It is an ego-based, win/lose management relationship in which you supervise others (or sometimes yourself) closely, monitor what they do and whether they are doing it effectively, reward them if they are effective, and assign consequences if they are not effective. Behavioral management creates compliance or noncompliance without regard to whether anyone enjoys it or not.

In a more enlightened management situation, however, you consider awakening a person's sense of personal integrity and his willingness to guide himself with integrity, so he manages his own behaviors. This is called promise based management. An employee has three possible responses to a manager's request to create a promise based management outcome:

- He can agree. He gives his promise or word. Assuming he has a healthy relationship with integrity, the manager trusts that promise unless the employee proves untrustworthy. He can say, "Yes, I will do it." That means he agrees to the four conditions of a proper request: specific, direct, measurable, and with a time frame attached to it.
- He can decline, saying "I won't do it." A discussion can follow to learn why and whether or not the manager needs to impose behavioral management or renegotiate the request.
- He can offer a counter request. One or more of the four conditions are modified.

A promise based management relationship creates self-empowered trust between people and a sense of *commitment* rather than compliance.

In a prison, for example, where you need compliance, behavioral management is appropriate. However, where you want people supporting each other, you want commitment, and promise based management is more effective in these situations. It creates an environment of mutual support, personal commitment, and empowered people applying themselves to a shared vision. However, be aware that this can only occur in an environment where people can be trusted to manage their own behaviors. The first step is to create an environment of willingness to operate with integrity rather than selfishness, along with the obvious requirement of having people who are capable of managing their own behaviors while operating in alignment with their promises, their honor, and their word.

As you execute your road map, who will help you and in what capacity?

Is it possible to practice promise based management? If so, how will you do this?

Perceptions of Reality

What does your perception of reality have to do with creating a road map from your current reality to your inspired future? Everything! Your perception of reality (or your conscious and unconscious mental model) includes the images, assumptions, and stories that make up your paradigm of reality. That paradigm, or the largest context that you are capable of considering, is the defining world that limits what you believe is possible.

Accordingly, your perception of reality limits how you see where you are, limits what you believe you are capable of achieving in the future, and most importantly, what the possible road maps are to reach that future. So, before you jump into creating your road map, you need to look more deeply at your perception of reality to determine how to best expand that foundation and create the optimal path from where you are to where you want to be.

Are perceptions accurate reflections of your direct experience or merely flawed interpretations of that experience?

David Hume (1711-1776), the famous Scottish philosopher, wrestled with this question. In his words, "When I enter most intimately into what I call myself, I always stumble on some particular impression or other, of heat or cold, light or shade, love or hatred, pain or pleasure. I never can catch myself without a perception, and never can observe any thing but the perception."

Hume concluded that we can only experience life through perception—which is clarified, labeled, and characterized through language or "inner dialogue"—and we can never directly experience true reality.

I don't know if Hume was correct. I do know that I and all my family, friends, and clients experience their reality through a constant stream of thoughts and inner dialogue that colors the interpretation of reality. The tone of that dialogue may be positive or negative, inspired or depressed, loving or disgusted, bored or stimulated. But whatever the tone, it completely determines the quality of that person's perceived current reality. Therefore, you could say that it determines reality itself.

Where do these thoughts come from that make up our inner dialogue? Do we have any influence over them?

Absolutely!

Sometimes certain overriding physical influences (chemical, physiological, or extreme psychological) may predominate. But most of the time, we let our stream of thoughts happen on their own as pure, unchallenged reactions to the present.

Most of us are conditioned to react to our immediate environment from a survival instinct, and we rarely disengage that reaction. Our inner dialogue streams forth in a constant reaction to our immediate circumstances, which tends to make us either emotional reactors or passive observers about future events. We get so comfortable reacting to our current reality that we unconsciously stop impacting those events.

If you desire to positively guide your experience of life, you must challenge this process, and *choose* to impact what happens next to have a definite influence on what actually *does* happen next! By shifting your perception from passive commentator to active anticipator, you take control of your process of perception and actually start impacting the upcoming reality.

Not only can you influence your perception of reality, you can actually change reality itself.

Many cancer victims have experienced spontaneous remission through visualization and many kids from impoverished backgrounds end up as millionaires in baseball, football, or basketball. Alexander Hamilton started out as a poor child from a Caribbean island and ended up as a founder of our country. Gandhi persuaded the British to relinquish hundreds of years of colonial rule in India.

Call it the power of faith, positive thinking, psycho-cybernetics, or self-hypnosis. You develop a vision of what you desire in the future, like a lighthouse of personal life vision that acts as a beacon. It becomes a powerful source of inspiration and passion that keeps you focused on growing nearer to it. It can be a concentrated representation of your deepest core values. It can be a flame that draws you like a moth to your greatest personal destiny.

But it only works if you have one and you stay committed to it.

Now you can decide if you want to do something about taking control of your future through this model or stay a passive observer of current reality like a victim of circumstance. And you are not the only one who has this decision to make. I do too. Each of us must make this decision every day, every time we are conscious, for as long as we live. It is the difference between being fully alive and going through life being simply "not dead."

Formula of Truth

Have you noticed that although information is available, it isn't necessarily used effectively? Many of us can learn advanced concepts, but have a gap in our ability to use the information to our advantage.

In the workplace, people don't always work efficiently, even when the information is available. They often refuse to use a process that works better than the one they are currently using.

Someone may hear an inspirational message and acknowledge it as a new way of thinking or acting, yet refuse to adopt it.

Why?

I created a formula to address these frustrations. It is simple to say and understand, but not easy to practice. The formula is this:

Concept + Experience = Truth (Ownership)

Here is how you use it. You have an exciting new idea to share with a friend about working out and losing weight. You tell him about the great book you read, the tremendous results he might experience from it, and your absolute testimonial that it will help him lose weight and be vibrant. What does he do? Nod politely and review the evening's television schedule in his mind while pretending to listen to you.

If you approach it differently, you might have different results. People have a built-in filter against acting on concepts. With the amount of data our brains are subjected to daily, we *must* filter out most of it or go insane! To circumvent the filtering and indifference of your audience when you present a new concept to them, you use the other half of the formula.

In the case of our inactive friend, you might approach the situation through experience before you introduce concept. Take him for a walk and make it enjoyable. Playfully engage him in lifting weights with you and see how he feels after he actually uses some of his muscles. Make him a wonderful dinner that tastes great and is low in calories. Help him experience the truth of the concept before trying to sell it to him. If he can experience the truth of your idea, and then you back it up with the foundational concept, he might find that what you are saying is true for him.

We all have excellent radar systems that filter what we allow ourselves to know is "true" for us. The only way we allow new truth into our lives is to experience it and understand it. Then we have the necessary tools to incorporate it into our self-concept and begin practicing it as though it is a rational part of us. The new truth must be owned or it will be dismissed as just another interesting concept.

You can explain to an employee why it is important to approach customers a certain way. That employee nods and smiles and can be engaged or not, but once he is in a situation with a customer and uses what he was trained to do—and it works—only then has he actually embraced it.

Try it with someone, even yourself. The next time you learn an interesting concept that is outside your comfort zone, try it anyway. Experience it, don't just filter it out.

Write down a situation in which you are trying to convince someone to see something your way and are failing. How can you use Concept + Experience = Truth (Ownership) to help that person internalize the new concept? Write down your plan.

Pyramid of Empowerment

As you build your road map, remember the mind-set discussion from Step 1. The Pyramid of Empowerment tool can help you overcome despondency or negative thoughts by shifting your thinking whenever necessary.

Let's say you wake up one day aware of your attitude (the third level) and think, *I'm in a bad mood. I feel depressed.* An attitude can last from a few minutes to a few months. In this sort of disempowered attitude, you are stagnant and depressed and usually not motivated to take any real action. Even if you can muster the energy to initiate action, you are easily discouraged if the action is not effective and quickly fall back into non-action, which further reinforces your disempowered attitude and deepens your stagnancy. A more effective way to overcome this state is to use the Pyramid of Empowerment.

Here's how to use it. The Pyramid of Empowerment creates solidity from bottom to top. When you feel disempowered, circle to the bottom and challenge the language or mind-set that is creating your thoughts. Remember that thoughts come from your mind-set— the language of your mind.

If you feel pessimistic, for example, go to the language level and ask yourself how a more empowered language or mind-set would sound at this moment. Further, ask what an optimistic thought might sound like at this moment. Generate new thoughts to shift your attitude. You are far more likely to take action and succeed from the resulting new attitude of optimism. Even if you have a setback at the action level, you are better able to ignore it and take corrective action (the fifth level).

As you move up, you correct your actions, which over time become skills that are more solid than mere corrective actions. The higher you go, the more these become permanent. Skills are areas of unconscious competence. Your skills determine your level of empowerment in the world, the light shining out the top of the pyramid.

For example, a new golfer approaches the first tee and feels afraid, knowing people are watching from the clubhouse. His attitude is doubtful; he may not even swing the club. If he does swing and the ball flies into the bushes, he might think he hears people laugh, get discouraged, and quit.

But if he notices he is doubtful and substitutes the language of possibility, he generates thoughts like: *Even Tiger Woods began with a first swing. The best golfers make mistakes. I win by getting a little better each time. I enjoy this game for the one or two good hits. I have nothing to lose. Let me just flow with it.* With that attitude of possibility, he swings. The swing is more likely to be successful. If it goes right or left, the pro might offer advice. He takes corrective action and plays more rounds. Over time he develops unconscious competence playing golf.

I only play golf once or twice a year, but I know I'll shoot in the 80s. I won't embarrass myself. I don't worry about it, think about it, or even practice any more. That empowers me to play golf whenever I wish and enjoy it.

Why do I mention my golf game to you? Because you have your own version of my golf game you can adjust. I hope you use the Pyramid of Empowerment to immediately and effectively improve all the games in your life.

The Limitations of Labels

Every time you meet someone, you filter them through your internal label machine and spit out a label. It might be either positive or negative—racist, sexist, ageist, political, sexual, loving, or hateful. All these labels, good or bad, accomplish two things:

- They separate that person from you.
- They limit what that person can be to you.

Next a value is placed on the label, judging the person superior or inferior, better or worse, friend or foe. After filtering and sorting, you may smugly sit back and listen to the rest of his sentence as he finishes introducing himself. You may think you now know him. He becomes the label you assign him.

The more you believe that labels define the entire person, the more you limit what that person can represent in your business, relationship, or life. If a manager limits people in such ways, he robs himself of accessing the full potential of those he labels. If a leader limits people in such ways, he limits their potential contribution to the vision, and therefore, to the vision itself. If a friend or spouse limits people in such ways, that person limits the love that can be given or received.

People are always infinitely more than the labels we assign them, if we only look more deeply at them and their lives. This concept of the limitations of labels is important because your mind-set about labels will serve to either help or hinder you as you create and execute an effective road map from your current reality to your inspired future. After all, other people are usually a critical part of any successful road map, and to avoid the limitations of labels allows the optimization of those people.

Think of someone you labeled in the past and what you later learned that made you abandon the label. When did labeling someone limit what happened? Review your plan and look for labels you can eliminate. What did you find?

The Art of the Plan

An interviewer once asked Tiger Woods' new golf coach, Hank Haney, "Was it intimidating for you to be asked to coach the greatest golfer in history?"

Haney answered, "Not really. I believe that a person can do almost anything if he has a plan and executes it. If someone creates a plan and executes it, he grows, and everyone—even Tiger— needs to grow."

How could you dramatically improve your relationship with the planning process and its execution—and, impact *your* growth? What comes to mind when you hear the word "plan"? Do you become intrigued? Bored? Anxious? Indifferent?

Planning is an incredibly important and valuable tool of personal power when used properly, yet people have many different reactions to it. Your reaction probably reveals your mental model, or subconscious assumptions, about what it means. Your perceived meaning largely determines how effectively you use this tool in your life.

Good planning begins with your mental model[10] about how you view plans. There are two general types of people when it comes to planning:

- The Methodicals
- The Improvisers

The Methodicals

Some people live by their plans. They have a budget for personal finance, a business plan at work, a workout plan for their health, a health insurance plan for their protection, and a grocery list pinned to their dashboard before they go to the store.

---

[10] My favorite definition for the term "Mental Model" is Peter Senge's, as presented in *The Fifth Discipline:* "Mental models are deeply held internal images of how the world works, images that limit us to familiar ways of thinking and acting. Very often, we are not consciously aware of our mental models or the effects they have on our behavior."

These people use plans as a structured, empirical guidance system for virtually everything they do. They approach plans with an almost reverential relationship that borders on worship, and could not operate without one. They think of planning as a kind of science and are usually quite effective in managing their lives.

Is there any downside to this approach? How creative or spontaneous are these people? They are often neither, because such spontaneity can be construed as "off-plan," or even a competing commitment to the plan. Such heresy is unconsciously considered counterproductive to the outcomes desired by the plan.

In cases where a structured approach represses creativity or out-of-the-box thinking, it can eventually cause stagnancy of growth. Methodicals are often found in jobs that reward careful and measurable progress, such as engineering, accounting, education, and real estate development. In organizations, they often show up as CFOs, COOs, CEOs, and effective middle managers.

The Improvisers

Some people don't live by predetermined plans. In fact, they abhor planning because it requires rehearsing situations or scenarios before they actually occur, determining a viable course of commitment and action, and holding themselves accountable to meeting certain deadlines. Improvisers tell themselves that they love the challenge of accomplishing something in the final hour and don't want to be restricted by inflexible plans.

Improvisers tend to be procrastinators, relationship oriented, personality oriented, and relatively self-confident. They can often be found in jobs that reward these types of attributes such as sales, marketing, politics, and public relations. They show up in organizations as charismatic or visionary leaders, but are rarely effective managers.

Neither type is superior. They each have strengths and weaknesses relative to effectiveness. For example, I have coached clients who were Methodicals and wonderful at planning, but poor at execution. Or, they were strong at both planning and execution, but lacked creative possibilities in the plans they made, sometimes resulting in uninspired growth or results. They are sometimes viewed as mere academics who spend too much time talking and not enough time acting.

I have also seen the downside, in terms of effectiveness, of Improvisers. These people are sometimes so spontaneous, so exhilarated by saving situations in the final hour, that they create anxiety and stress in many of their teammates. The teammates then wonder if they will pull it off or suffer the brunt of vitriol from angry customers who feel vulnerable to the lack of methodical progress or communication. Procrastination and reactive actions limit the effectiveness of Improvisers, so they end up feeling constantly stressed or under the gun.

Artful Planning As an Alternative

The third method does not make planning a burdensome and uninspired process for widget counters and boring managers (two of the negative perceptions that Improvisers may have about Methodicals), nor does it give in to the serendipitous and ineffective impulse of just "winging it" and hoping for effective execution (which is often the perception that Methodicals have about Improvisers).

This method doesn't make planning a science, but an art.

If you treat planning as a simple, necessary vehicle for getting what you want, on your own terms and time frame, it becomes an opportunistic tool rather than a tool of oppression. Think of planning as your way of getting out of any problem you currently face, as well as your way of getting something you desire that you don't currently have. Think of planning as fun—yes, fun!

Artful planning includes seven critical elements:

1. A written, structured road map for realizing your desired outcome.
2. Components of that road map are large and inclusive enough to incorporate:
    *   The values you are committed to practicing in the plan (i.e., integrity, win/win results, etc.)
    *   A brief overview of the optimal outcome in brief, clear terms
    *   The goals necessary to achieve that optimal outcome
    *   Milestones to track progress toward each goal including specific, direct, measurable outcomes with time frames attached
    *   Specific short-term, intermediate, and long-term actions to reach the milestones
3. A clear determination of necessary resources, including the team members needed to achieve success with the artful plan.
4. Time set aside to create the plan, as well as to monitor it.
5. Opportunities within the creation and execution of the plan for leadership, management, and coaching.
6. Opportunities within the creation and execution of the plan for personal and circumstantial barriers to be encountered and overcome, creating personal growth.
7. Appropriate flexibility within the plan for modification to improve its results and desired outcomes.

Designed and executed this way, artful planning can become a creative force in your life and the life of your organization, used to realize your ultimate future potential, rather than to merely remind you of past failures. If you use plans this way, as tools of growth rather than tools of self-repression or punishment, they can be delightful and critical vehicles for helping you attain the happiness you desire and deserve.

Following the next section, you will use the Echo of Empowerment tool to create your road map.

The Alchemy of Perspective: Converting Adversity into Purposeful Empowerment

Alchemy is the ancient pseudoscience of turning lead into gold. The "scientists" of the Middle Ages believed they could change base metals into precious ones using various chemical and mystical approaches. To my knowledge, they never succeeded. However, alchemy is a useful metaphor to convert something from one state into another, such as from a place of worthlessness and pain into a place of value and power.

Let's apply the idea of alchemy to our minds and perspectives on life and business.

As a business coach, I explore the underlying issues in people's lives, business challenges, and careers. I notice that often no relationship exists between a person's circumstances and how he experiences that place. Some people experience misery during wonderful circumstances; conversely, others experience contentment and joy in adverse circumstances.

Therein lies my first inquiry into the alchemy of perspective.

Adversity is the easiest place to see this dynamic at work. During the housing bust and mortgage fiascos of 2008 and 2009, we could have easily declared this reality: The mortgage industry was being devastated. Many companies went out of business; many employees lost their jobs.

However, other people in the real estate and mortgage industries were thriving. They were busier than ever, and growing their businesses in new and exciting ways that would lay the groundwork for a much larger market share in the years to come.

How could this be? Doesn't reality have to impact us all? The answer lies in how individuals viewed the market. Those who did not accept the interpretation of adversity being reality chose to see:

- a longer time frame to what was happening
- why it happened, without the guilt or paralysis of continuing to be a contributor to those causes
- what wasn't working and how to avoid practicing ineffective activities, processes, or mind-sets in the future
- how cycles work, and how to have faith that the cycle of that moment would work that way, too
- the opportunity to go back to basics, to develop and execute an objective action plan, courageously express their core values, and not sell out to their fears
- the chance to be a visionary leader in a world of reactive managers, and to lead the charge toward an inspirational (if not entirely predictable or controllable) future
- the requirement for courageous action in the service of a greater good, and the need to grow themselves and their organizations beyond the temptations of waiting for someone else to give them the answer

The answer for a person in any adverse climate (job loss, self-destructive family members, health challenges, or personal economic uncertainty) is to become an alchemist of his own perspective. Doing so is one step towards taking responsibility for his future.

You can convert the "lead" of today's fears and uncertainties into the "gold" of tomorrow's outcomes by controlling what you look at and by committing to a game plan that moves you toward the promised land of tomorrow's possibilities. This takes courage, vision, faith, inspiration, creativity, and confidence in the future, in others, and in yourself.

The skeptics, cynics, and fear-based people may think you are like Don Quixote tilting at windmills when you talk about optimistic opportunities or bright tomorrows. Ignore them. More importantly, forgive them, for they are responding to negative and fearful mind-sets generated by the constant barrage of negative nightly news stories that tell us why we must be afraid and paralyzed with uncertainty.

Many others have known and practiced the alchemical approach:

- Warren Buffett only buys stocks when others are selling, and by doing so, has made himself one of the wealthiest men in the world.
- Mahatma Gandhi transformed India and became a worldwide figure of love, compassion, courage, and truth.
- Thomas Edison failed countless times before he developed the electric lightbulb.
- Abraham Lincoln went bankrupt multiple times in business before becoming one of our greatest presidents.
- Viktor Frankl, a Jew, survived the Holocaust by practicing exactly what we are discussing here.
- Our parents and grandparents suffered through two world wars and the Great Depression, yet pulled together and sacrificed their comfort—and even their lives—so we could have the opportunities we have today.
- Someone in your life encouraged you when you were ready to give up.

In the end, it doesn't matter how safe or comfortable we were along the journey. Who we are when we face challenges determines our worthiness for power and fulfillment. The goal is to overcome adversity with courage and resolve, instead of returning to a former state of perceived comfort, control, or predictability.

The process of personal alchemy begins by taking responsibility for your perspective and expanding that perspective until you can envision a future you desire. As long as you envision inspired outcomes, create a systematic road map to reach that future, and then execute that road map, it is only a matter of time until you arrive there.

You can only execute this process and create different outcomes if you use your core values as your guidance system.

Your comfort is about what you were and had in the past. Your values are about your commitment to yourself and others for the future, even in the presence of fear. As the saying goes, "Adversity doesn't create character, it reveals it."

Echo of Empowerment

The Echo of Empowerment (E of E) is a simple and powerful method to systematically create anything you want. Please visit www.integrativemasteryprograms.com/book/downloads.htm and print several copies of the Echo of Empowerment worksheet as you will update it every thirty days. You may have several projects going at once. Write the name of your project on the line at the bottom of the figure.

You already determined which current reality you want to change (Step 2) and made creative tension by envisioning the future (Step 3). Enter the current reality details (what is and isn't working) in the left-hand oval and the desired outcome (Personal Life Vision) in the right-hand oval using bullet points.

In the third column, write short-term goals that will measure progress in the next thirty days. Start at the bottom of Column 3 and declare your intangible goals, such as "feel more energetic and happy." In the top three boxes, write measurable, tangible goals such as "lose five pounds by Dec. 30," and "reduce my cholesterol by 5% by Dec. 30."

In the second column, create specific, direct, measurable actions with time frames to execute over the next ten days that will allow you to reach the goals you declared in Column 3.

This brief overview captures the essential components of the Echo of Empowerment project accomplishment process. The following may help you understand it more clearly so you can craft your road maps today and in the future.

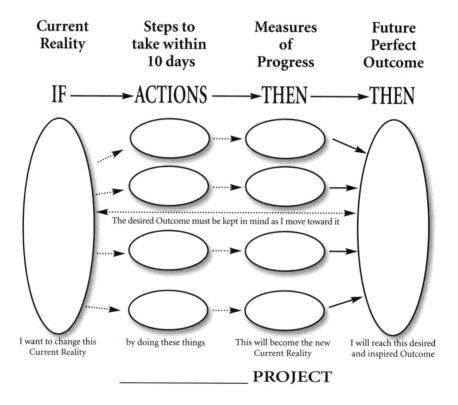

Example:

Column 1: I am unhealthy, sickly, and have no energy.

Column 4: I am vibrant. I have ample health for the rest of my life and tremendous energy. I can do anything I want to do.

Column 3: I will lose ten pounds, lower my body fat by 7%, and walk three miles a day (tangible). I will feel better about myself, look better to others, look trimmer (intangible, subjective feelings).

Column 2: Starting today and continuing for at least 6 months, I walk ½ hour, 3 days a week and measure the distance I cover. I record everything I eat and choose food with less fat.

Using the Echo of Empowerment for Large Projects

Use this technique to create both large and small projects. A huge project, known as a macro-project, is broken down into a series of micro-projects, which are more manageable. For example, if health is your macro-project (as described above), micro-projects might be: diet, cardiovascular health, flexibility and strength, and mental health.

Create one sheet for the macro-project and for each micro-project. On the macro-project sheet, complete the first and fourth columns, since the actions needed (column 2) will be detailed on each of the smaller projects. The micro-project names will be the milestones (column 3) on the macro-project sheet because completing the micro-projects automatically fulfills the macro-project.

Work closely with your coach to successfully develop and execute your projects. Your projects are the crucible of developing your ultimate empowerment and results.

The Echo of Empowerment is powerful and simple. It is a way to give yourself effective structure and accountability while still providing a systematic process for achieving results.

It may interest you to know how this simple tool was created. Years ago, I was awakened in the middle of the night by a dream. I had been ruminating for months over how to pay for my son's college tuition. I dreamed about this tool, got out of bed, and used it to solve the problem in five minutes! Then, feeling the momentum and growing confidence of having found a magical answer to all my problems, I asked myself *What else is bothering me that I want to stop worrying about?*

In the next ninety minutes I solved six more problems that had been on my mind. I had found a way to get things done simply, easily, and effectively. And, now so have you.

Looking Forward

Now you have your plan—your big picture macro-plan and a series of bite sized micro-plans. As you start to work through them, however, you will undoubtedly encounter obstacles and barriers.

That is the topic of the next chapter.

STEP 5

Barriers

What one believes to be true either is true or becomes true within limits to be found experientially and experimentally; these limits are beliefs to be transcended.

— John Lilly

Once your road map is in place, the next step is to execute it. But doesn't something always seem to get in the way of your well laid plans?

We use the word "barrier" to identify *anything* that could prevent you from effectively executing any of the first four steps (creating a values based mind-set, analyzing current reality, creating an inspirational future, and creating an effective road map). Step 5 helps you identify those barriers. In the next chapter, we will discuss how to break through them.

For example, let's use the health analysis again. I decide that I want to get in great shape, be healthy, and have vibrancy until I am a hundred years old. I put together a road map for an aerobic exercise program and strength and flexibility training. It details which foods I will eat and avoid, blood work, and a physician who monitors everything. I join the gym, have my equipment, and I am ready to go.

However, when I analyze the barriers, I realize that I have an internal barrier of self-doubt because I have tried these things before and did not succeed. This barrier from my past sabotages my confidence that I can actually achieve my goal. An external barrier is that the health club is far enough away that I am not sure I can get there every morning. If I cannot afford to buy weights, that is also a barrier.

These ideas are not meant to discourage you, but to help you be realistic about the obstructions you may meet along the road, before they become roadblocks. Being prepared helps you circumnavigate obstacles, rather than being stopped in your tracks by them.

This chapter contains several tools that will help you identify barriers, both internal and external.

Identify Your Barriers

On the left side of a page in your journal or on the worksheet page you download from www.integrativemasteryprograms.com/book/downloads.htm, list any internal barriers that might get in the way of executing your plan. These include doubts, beliefs, thoughts, or anything else that would reduce your commitment. On the right, note what you might do to remove that barrier.

On the left side, list any external barriers that might get in the way of executing your plan. These include conflicting projects, time or space barriers, or anything else that would get between you and your goal. Put the possible solutions on the right.

List the personality tendencies that might stand in your way, including habits, addictions, or other behaviors that distract you from your goals.

List any other internal, mental, emotional, or psychological barriers or beliefs that could get in your way.

Think about the other people you will depend on to reach your goal. What conflicts or differences exist between you that might get in the way of achieving your goal such as conflicting commitments, personality tendencies, strengths, styles, behaviors, or beliefs?

Hope vs. Commitment: The Critical Choice

How much time do you spend hoping? We often think of hope as a positive feeling, at least as an alternative to despair. However, there is no real power in merely hoping that things get better. Examine these statements:

The stock market tumbles—	"I sure hope it comes back."
My kid is on drugs—	"I sure hope he gets off them."
My job is at risk—	"I hope they don't fire me."
My blood pressure is too high—	"I hope I bring it down before I have complications."

It is easy to settle for hope when dealing with life's problems—much easier than actually taking action to fix them. Hope places the power of resolution outside of us in the external world. An empowered, effective approach for overcoming adversity is commitment. Commitment creates personal responsibility for dealing with business, health, relationship, or life problems in an active and confident way, rather than a passive and victimized way.

Commitment alone helps you modify your future.

Here is an example. The Ritz-Carlton Hotel chain wants to be viewed as the most customer-service oriented hotel chain in the world. Can they achieve that vision by merely hoping it happens? No. Instead, they authorize every employee to "own" any customer service problem that arises until it is solved. No one dismisses a problem. If a maid discovers that a customer hates his room, it is her responsibility to solve the problem and satisfy the customer. Furthermore, every employee is authorized to spend up to $2,000 of the organization's money to solve any customer service problem without approval from any manager.

Do you see the difference between active commitment and passive hope?

Let's look at the earlier examples through the same eyes:

- The stock market tumbles: You commit to a plan that takes advantage of the lower stock prices and simultaneously diversifies your portfolio so you are less vulnerable to future volatility.
- Your child is on drugs: You commit to an intervention or an effective program of treatment, communication, support, education, and consequences until he gains the maturity to make better decisions.
- Your job is at risk: You could commit to changing your productivity, time management, or attitude so you become too valuable for them to lose. Alternatively, you might find a new career or start your own company.
- Your blood pressure is too high: Commit to an exercise and diet plan that you follow. Stop acting helpless and doubting yourself. Adjust your mind-set to empowered self-esteem and self-appreciation.

Review the list of barriers you wrote from the exercise on page 96. Do any of the actions you listed in the right-hand column rely on hope? How can you convert them into committed actions?

Integrity Is Good Business

Phil had a problem. As a small businessman who handled the database for a recent Olympics, he became aware of inappropriate expenditures by the Olympic Fundraisers Committee. They had wasted huge sums of money entrusted to them by investors who had expected to profit from the housing for these games. Phil knew what was going on, and he was an honorable man who was incapable of going along with the graft. He simply could not live with himself if he looked the other way.

Phil went to the committee and said that he expected them to tell the investors what was happening. They thought he was crazy. They offered to bribe him. Since he had invested virtually all of his company's resources in this venture, he faced the loss of his business by going against them.

They said, "Take our deal and we'll see that you get 100 percent of your money back, but tell the investors and you'll go down with them."

He talked to his wife about it. He prayed about it. No matter how he looked at it, he knew he had only one choice. He had to be a man of integrity and tell the other investors, even if it cost him his business. He told the investors the next day and they confronted the committee, who excused the situation as beyond their control and simply a poor investment. The enterprise went bust.

But something amazing happened. The investors were so impressed with Phil's integrity, they found out all they could about his business and started recommending him to everyone they knew. When his payroll was threatened, an investor randomly called him, learned of the situation, and covered it, with easy repayment terms.

Today, Phil is a wealthy man because his commitment to principles outweighed his doubt and fear.

Sometimes we have to remind ourselves that in addition to all the other great benefits that it has, integrity is also good business.

Review your list of barriers again. Could any be removed or mitigated by increasing your level of integrity?

Authentic Dialogue

An easy way to identify barriers is to create a real conversation or dialogue. Use open-ended questions and a back-and-forth interchange of ideas with a trusted colleague or friend. See if you arrive at a greater collective sensibility than you could by simply declaring what you each already believe. Listen empathetically and really notice what the other person says. Discover what barriers are present to your understanding of each other, and write them down.

Next, create a dialectical process of understanding. This tool, developed by the nineteenth century philosopher Georg Wilhelm Friedrich Hegel, proposes that something is "true," creating a thesis. From that thesis, its natural opposite, or antithesis, is created. From the tension of these opposing truths, the best components of each are merged, resulting in a synthesis. This synthesis, Hegel believed, becomes a new thesis, starting the process anew. Thus, this process of thesis → antithesis → synthesis → thesis was Hegel's description of how things evolve to better and better forms.

A dialogue, then, is a form of elevated understanding achieved when people contribute ideas to one another and create this dialectical process of understanding.

Practice your version of a dialogue with someone today. Notice where you want to jump in and say what you think, convince, or argue. This is a competing monologue, usually the norm in conversation. Instead, don't interrupt. Do ask open-ended questions and be sincerely interested to see if you can arrive at a higher understanding of the topic. Ask the other person to do the same in their part of your dialogue. This is authentic conversation.

Directing Your Tapes and Movie

With the negative drama of daily life inundating us from the television and newspapers, problems at work, and relationship challenges, how do we ever feel joy and peace? Where do we find the power to be happy?

We need to change our point of view. We are all in our own "movie" all the time, and everyone else is a supporting actor in that movie. Further, we each tend to believe that our movie is The Movie and we spend much of our lives promoting, justifying, and trying to convince others of that belief. This is a primary cause of interpersonal conflicts, such as war and divorce. The figure below illustrates this.

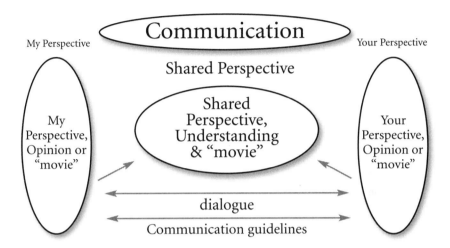

This truth gives us power over our past, future, relationships, and actions. To forget it is to doom ourselves to merely react to external circumstances and fight with others over whose "movie" is correct. But even if we react, we can remember something else and regain our power: *The tape in my mind about this experience determines the effectiveness of my reaction and all outcomes.*

With control over how we perceive the events of our lives, we can effectively impact them.

Many of my clients face tremendous life challenges. Some handle them well; others are completely foiled by them. The single greatest variable that explains their different responses is whether or not the person remembers that he controls his personal life movie.

Some people respond to tremendous adversity with noble courage, intrinsic faith, and absolute resolve. Others melt down at the first sign of trouble.

Do you act offended when someone says something critical about you?

I had a business partner for ten years who had been a close friend for many years before that. While building our business, we went through countless trials. We overcame them all. However, the relationship grew toxic over time. Eventually, he asked me to find a buyer so we could cash out and end our business partnership. His final words were terribly hurtful and personally offensive. I walked away from the relationship feeling great sadness and pain.

My perspective on that final interaction has evolved over the years since.

- My immediate reaction to his attack was indignation and anger, followed by the gathering of evidence as to why he was "wrong" and I was "right." I felt martyred.
- Over the years, shared employees told me he never wanted to sell but I had forced him to. I felt unfairly judged by others and, of course, martyred.
- Then something interesting happened. Over the last few years, as I helped hundreds of people resolve their own relationship breakdowns and barriers, I began to see it differently. While coaching, I exercise the power to control my tapes and my movie by filtering them through my values, principles, and personal life vision. As I grew more used to identifying with those values and principles, I changed my interpretation of my former friend and business partner.
- In his movie, he interpreted my actions differently than how I interpreted them. No "right" or "wrong" existed, but we each told ourselves "I am right and he is wrong."
- We kept those interpretations alive with the tapes we played in our minds about what the other did or said and we began the inevitable gathering of negative

evidence to bolster our judgments. We never challenged those conclusions. We let the evidence build, resulting in terminal breakdown of the relationship.

But we could have handled it differently.

Communication

Had we effectively communicated our personal views on the partnership, we may have reached a different outcome, such as:
- understanding why the other person felt as he did and gaining some measure of empathy
- expressing that empathy, modifying what we did, and remaining committed to the friendship
- Saving a twenty-year friendship instead of throwing it away, along with future growth opportunities

The pathway to sharing our movies and tapes to prevent the tragedy of broken relationships is effectively to understand those movies. It isn't enough to *tell* the other person about *your* movie and tapes. You have to *understand* them before perfect communication can occur.

What gives us the resolve and awareness to want to understand other people's movies? Principle-based identity instead of ego-based identity. If we commit to expressing our principles and values, instead of promoting our personalities and ego, we gain the power of true empathy and purpose. With that power, we become less attached to being "right," and operate more effectively.

A full-sized version of this worksheet may be found at www.integrativemasteryprograms.com/book/downloads.htm
1. Think back on the movie of your life. List three events that could have had better outcomes had you practiced these ideas.

2. Write the impact that this awareness could have on your future.

3. Are you gathering evidence against anyone right now? What judgmental or critical tapes are you running about other people?

4. Are you running any tapes about your company or business?

5. Are you running any tapes about your finances?

6. Are you running any tapes about your health?

7. Are you running any tapes about your spirituality?

8. What changes will you make as a result of this exercise?

Please take this advice from someone who suffered the repercussions of too many years of ego-based living and the loss of too many relationships, and use this information to transform your life: Challenge your tapes and movies; replace the ineffective ones with ones that reflect truth, love, empathy, and forgiveness.[11] The following exercise will help you practice.

Practice Directing Your Tapes and Movies

To reinforce this new habit, try the following exercise. The next time you are in a conversation that involves disagreement, remind yourself that the person you are talking to is in his own movie and you are just a walk-on player in it. Listen as if you are in his movie instead of defending your own. Recognize that he is expressing and living out his movie and be curious about it. See if you are inspired and excited by how you see your relationship through his point of view. Look for solutions he might find, which could be different from your own.

[11] For an excellent tool to help you practice this critically important tool, read *Make Me an Instrument of Your Peace*, by Kent Nerburn, 1999.

Next, share what you have been doing. Then share your movie of the situation, explaining how it is different than his. Point out that neither is better or right, they are just different. Invite him to join you in your movie and ask him how he now sees the situation. Introduce him to the idea that we limit ourselves by only viewing life through our own movies.

Converting Addictions

Does the word "addiction" create the negative connotation of tragic behavior in yourself or others? What if addictions did not have to be the enemy, but could be a source of growth and empowerment?

Human beings are intrinsically addictive in their approach to life. We generally consider addictions to be negative. In doing so, we may prevent ourselves from exploring how we could use our intrinsic addictive tendencies to regenerate our lives and businesses.

The dictionary defines addiction in many ways, one of which is "habituation." Could your habitual practices be positive?

Some positive habits or addictions that a person could have include:

- exercise
- yoga
- spiritual practices
- healthy diet
- saying affirmations, aloud or silently
- loving other people
- solid work ethic
- accountability
- creating inspirational thoughts for ourselves or others

These are all states of operating that often become habituated in our daily lives, and which can regenerate those lives.

What are some negative addictions that degenerate your life or those of others?

- poor diet
- negative thinking
- poor or nonexistent exercise practices
- gossip
- fear
- hateful attitude
- laziness
- alcohol or drug abuse
- poor self-image
- selfishness

Are our addictions imposed on us from our parents, teachers, or other experiences in our lives? What if we have much greater control over our addictions than we typically give ourselves credit for?

Addictions are habits, pure and simple. If you are a cigarette smoker, for instance, you can blame your physical craving for cigarettes on an "addiction" to not only the chemicals in them, but also to the feeling you get by smoking them. But you still choose to respond to those cravings by picking up a cigarette. You don't lose the choice, you lose the belief and willingness that you can make a better decision.

What are alternate choices to picking up a cigarette? Not picking it up and choosing to chew on a toothpick, going for a run, or doing another more beneficial habit that could eventually replace the act of smoking.

Will you go through "withdrawal" when you alter negative habits in favor of positive ones? Probably, but that is merely a measure of your commitment to operate in a more healthful future over the long term.

If a person can identify the addictions that do not serve the future he is committed to, identify positive alternatives to those negative addictions that regenerate power and life, and formulate a sincere commitment to practicing the new habits, then true control of the future can be obtained. This, in the end, is the essence of personal mastery.

The courage to replace degenerative habits with regenerative ones exemplifies the practice of operating from commitment rather than comfort. This approach to life makes a person eligible to create any future he desires.

The new regenerative habits have even more power if they also benefit other people. For example, I may decide to lose weight through diet and exercise. I will have more power to commit to that change if I do it so my grandchildren will know me some day, rather than to look better walking on the beach next month.

What are some unchallenged addictions that you practice? What do you do at work that doesn't serve your commitment to a principle-based approach to life? With your health? In your family life?

If you mastered yourself in this way, what impact might you have in inspiring others to take control of their own lives?

What will you do about converting your negative addictions to positive addictions this year?

Authentic Stewardship

On the eve of my oldest son returning from his first semester at college, my wife, younger son, and I prepared to greet him. However, due to ongoing challenges, I anticipated an uncomfortable scene.

Then a client called for his coaching session and shared a deeply personal story of an interaction he had with a customer who was going through great fear and anxiety. The customer revealed many details that could have sparked suspicion and major doubt in my client about his trustworthiness. As the conversation progressed, my client saw a choice to be judgmental and negative toward his customer or to practice compassion and understanding. He chose the latter. He listened to the customer until he finally saw his intrinsic integrity, and then acted in a way that changed his customer's life and restored his faith in fellow human beings.

Both of these situations involve a decision to operate beyond the limitations of individual ego and personality, from a place of authentic stewardship.

I asked my family to coach me to be kind to and understanding of our returning son, knowing that he had gone through a life transition. Despite the issues that angered and disappointed me, I decided to put aside my own inclination to "fight to be right." My wife and I love him and have committed to being stewards of his future. We want to support him in becoming the best person he can, over the long term.

Had we rolled out our list of complaints the moment we saw him at the airport, what would his response have been? If that were me, I would have run for the exit! Life at college would have seemed like my real home.

But we remembered that life is long, memories are longer, and that we loved and supported him. We remembered to be authentic stewards of our relationships so we could put first things first and make sure he knew that we loved him before we discussed potentially explosive issues. Practicing this approach allowed him to hear us more clearly and openly when we finally discussed the issues that upset us.

What about the client and his customer? My client was in the mortgage business and much of the preliminary evidence on the man's credit report and in his life story indicated he might be a risky customer. Instead of assuming that, my client listened to the customer's hopes, dreams, aspirations, and fears. He told the customer he wasn't ready for a home yet because he had to clear up some issues, but he would help him. Then, in a few months, when his credit had been repaired, he could get a loan he could afford.

As the interview continued, the customer began to trust my client and told him he was afraid of the future. My client practiced his Personal Life Vision values of faith and integrity, and asked the man to try having faith. He told him to trust the future, and that he would be an ally in supporting him toward that future, for him and his family. Sure, there would be tough times, but he now had a friend, advisor, and confidant who would be right there beside him.

The man virtually wept at the kindheartedness of my client, a complete stranger.

I could tell you many other stories to demonstrate this point. A dear friend and CFO of a Montana mortgage company had her life saved by a complete stranger after a near fatal accident in the middle of the night. The stranger happened to be trained as an emergency medical technician.

I have an inspirational friend who is a Harvard graduate and a genius in psychotherapy. He no longer needs to work, but chooses to help challenged and distraught people by restoring their faith in life.

All these people share one thing in common: a commitment to authentic stewardship. To be authentic means to be genuine or true. Stewardship (in a spiritual context) refers to the responsibility that people have to maintain and wisely use the gifts that God has given them.

An authentic steward, then, genuinely practices his unique gifts in relationship to other people, places, and things. An authentic steward is a values-driven person who manifests those values in situations to achieve the optimal outcome for all, not just for his own acknowledgment or benefit.

Whether you are a CEO or a receptionist, husband or wife, minister or atheist, man or woman, young or old, it is the same choice. It comes down to your heart, mind, and soul when you answer this question, posed internally to yourself: *Considering this person or situation, will I operate as an expression of my self-serving, self-validating ego or as a courageous expression of authentic stewardship by personifying my core values?*

Your answer to this question determines the outcome you achieve and something much more important: your eligibility to be empowered beyond your own intrinsic personal limitations to create the future you are capable of, unlimited by anything in your past.

Breaking Through Barriers that Hold Us Back

Bob was the sales manager on a team of managers. He knew he should have a solution to the problem of declining sales volume, but he didn't. Worse still, he was afraid the other team members would call him on his inadequacy and maybe even tell his boss. He wasn't trained in creative solutions at graduate school.

Bob's team felt increasingly anxious about the lack of sales, and the members had their own opinions about the problem. Many blamed themselves, but most blamed something or someone else. Soon the company would be in trouble. Each quietly suspected that he could have done something that might have prevented the situation from occurring.

Julie thought she wasn't smart enough to be on the team, and hoped nobody else had noticed. Ron thought Julie was the problem, but wasn't sure why. Betsy felt she lacked adequate experience to really face this problem, since she was a new manager. Joe blamed the sales staff, whom he judged to be lazy and unmotivated.

What is the common denominator in this management team?

One common theme is their relationship to their personal barriers. Each blames the problems on some external obstacle that has stopped him or her from moving forward to solve the problem. The obstacles seem insurmountable because they haven't been clarified. Everyone is afraid to face the barriers—or even identify them. They each want to do something helpful, but none considers that how he views his personal barriers has anything to do with the lack of a tenable solution. If they don't find a new perspective on the team's barriers, they are doomed to failure.

Circumstances such as an improved market climate might help, but they can't control or count on that. In fact, that's what many management teams do—hide their limitations and hope that circumstances bail them out.

How might breaking through the barriers resolve everyone's problem? Here is a possible thought sequence:

- To solve a problem, growth is required.
- For growth to occur, positive change is required.
- For positive change to occur, breakthroughs are required—new ways of doing things regardless of the past.
- For breakthroughs to occur, a barrier of some sort has to be overcome.
- For a barrier to be overcome, it needs to be acknowledged and identified.
- Desire is required to break through the barrier.

Desire can come from negative or positive motivation. Fears represent negative motivation. ("If I don't stop gaining weight, I'll have a heart attack.") Inspirational futures represent a positive motivation. ("I want to look great at the beach.") Negative motivators lose power as progress is made because the negative condition is erased. Positive motivators gain power as the goal grows bigger and stronger.

There are three primary keys to breaking through barriers:

1. Look for and identify barriers that are holding you back. Don't hide them or deny them.

2. Envision and articulate an inspirational outcome or future that you can't reach without breaking through the barrier.

3. Acknowledge the breakthrough once it occurs. Acknowledgement maintains the breakthrough and allows you to remain beyond the barrier.

To practice eliminating barriers takes conscious commitment. The outcome is growth in any of life's domains.

Review your barriers again. What is your desired outcome? What actions are you willing to take? How will you acknowledge your progress?

Your Stakeholders

Now that you understand the concept of authentic stewardship, consider those who benefit from your choices. For example, you are an employer. Your company has a mission to be a tremendously successful entity that provides great products to consumers. Your employees are direct stakeholders because they will have a place to work if the business is successful. The indirect stakeholders are your employees' families. They have a nice life from the income of your primary stakeholders, who benefit from the success of your mission.

When you identify your direct and indirect stakeholders, you magnify your perspective on the solutions you want. You naturally assume a greater mind-set of stewardship by anticipating the direct and indirect consequences of your solutions. This happens as a natural consequence of identifying your stakeholders.

You naturally and suddenly consider how your solutions will impact those people. Then you will tend to expand your solutions to more principled outcomes rather than self-interested ones.

Who has a direct stake in you being effective, successful, empowered, or inspirational? Identify them by name.

Who are your indirect stakeholders?

Review your list. Does everyone in the world benefit from your mission and your personal life vision and values? If not, your mission may be too small and you may be thinking too small. Revise, if necessary.

Looking Forward

Now that you have identified some barriers that may hold you back, the next step is to break through them. The next chapter will give you tools for doing just that.

STEP 6
Breakthroughs to Barriers

To understand Truth one must have a very sharp, precise, clear mind; not a cunning mind, but a mind that is capable of looking without any distortion, a mind innocent and vulnerable.
— Krishnamurti

How do you keep the barriers you identified in Step 5 from interfering with your road map and the other steps you have accomplished so far? To overcome your problems, you must break through them! This chapter will tell you how.

Internal, psychological breakthroughs might involve a coach, therapist, self-help book, affirmations, positive thoughts, prayer, meditation, or friends and family. All of these resources can help you overcome the mental models and paradigms and your own internal belief systems that are often the source of your barriers.

External barriers require more creativity to overcome. For example, if one of your barriers is that you cannot afford to buy exercise equipment, how could you exercise without buying equipment? For free, you can do heavy lifting, take a walk, or go for a jog. You can fill up buckets or bottles with water to use as weights. You can find used equipment or barter for what you need.

You need a breakthrough for every barrier to reduce its influence. Otherwise, barriers will stop you from starting on your road map or derail you soon after you start.

How to Put the Power Back into Your Life

Most people today create and live in a disempowered state regarding issues of power, trust, and commitment.

Your power is a direct reflection of how congruent your actions are with your core values and clarity of purpose. Trust is created when you act consistently with your stated purpose.

A person's word is his declaration of his truest promise, his purest expression of being. A person's promise is a powerful and sacred thing. When it is given, it should be so solid that anyone who hears it trusts that whatever has been promised will occur, to the absolute extent of the giver's ability to make it happen. Such a person is *whole*.

The opposite is a person who is *incongruent*. This person is disempowered and cannot be trusted to complete his commitments. He does not mean to be this way. In fact, he is often the most noble and well-intentioned of people, which is the problem: he treats commitments as mere intentions, thereby making them subject to non-fulfillment if his priorities change.

This person robs himself of power and trustworthiness. Others expect him to break his commitments. He is always late to appointments or meetings, and the world does nothing to prevent his disjunctive, incongruent behavior.

The sad reality is that people like this can't even trust themselves. They feel powerless and empty because they are unable to build a life that reflects their highest values.

Here is the difference:

Whole people:	Incongruent people:
show up at appointments or meetings on time or early	often show up late or cancel at the last minute
never make excuses for breaking their word	often make excuses for breaking their commitments
control their lives as much as any human being can	feel they have no control
are clear who they are and what they stand for	fear saying no to others (which results in even more over-commitment and disempowerment)
stand up for the core values and principles they believe in	feel self-conscious of their core values
are ruthless in controlling their calendars, commitments and circumstances	cannot be trusted when making commitments, even by themselves
follow through with what they say they will do	often grow discouraged about creating what they desire
have power to direct their lives with great certainty of the outcome	are controlled by circumstances
operate with a discernable air of control and calm, regardless of circumstances	often display a sense of anxiety or angst, as though they are barely in control

Which describes you better: whole or incongruent? What will you do to be more whole and less incongruent?

You are not doomed to being incongruent in the future even if you were in the past. In fact, you will experience a transformational epiphany if you declare yourself whole from now on, and hold yourself accountable.

The next tool will help you with this declaration, and your accountability.

Creating Opportunity from Adversity

I visit each leader's team at my workshops. One day, when I came to Steve's team, a charismatic lady was speaking. Her team members listened attentively, some with tears in their eyes and slight smiles on their faces.

Pat was an articulate, passionate woman, and I had noticed her earlier because she was engaged and responsive to the materials. She smiled readily, yet I saw a depth that told me she had a story to share. What an understatement!

"I've lived the majority of my life as a Type A personality," she declared to her little group. "I'm originally from Boston, and when I moved to Montana with my husband, I was driven by ambition and success. I went through people and problems rather than working with the relationships, and I might have operated from that arrogance forever had something huge not occurred." She paused for a moment, then continued. "My husband of forty-two years, Wally, was diagnosed with inoperable cancer."

The room grew quiet.

I felt myself girding for the sob story, the victim's tale of a truly sad situation that threatened to destabilize my own illusion that I wouldn't ever face such tragedy in my life. Everyone focused entirely on Pat, breath held in anticipation of what she would say next. Each of us dreaded the anticipated sadness and pain that she would undoubtedly reveal.

What she said, however, was something totally unexpected.

"Today, I'm a changed woman," she quietly declared. "Wally and I live each day, and each moment of the day, focused on the now. We live with an awareness of the preciousness of each moment that we never experienced before. Before you start feeling sorry for me, don't," she gently admonished. "I have two futures: one with Wally and one after Wally, and I'm working on making both of them inspirational. Wally and I discuss them openly and you probably won't believe what I'm about to tell you," she declared as she scanned the room, looking deeply into the eyes of those who would meet hers.

"Wally and I consider his terminal cancer to be the greatest blessing of our lives."

The room sat silent. No one really knew how to respond to that. I began to hope that perhaps she would conclude on a positive note.

"If Wally and I had a choice between him being totally healthy and exactly as we were before his cancer, without our current state of absolute gratitude, or him dying of cancer with both of us fully appreciating our lives, we would choose the cancer," she finished.

She smiled and looked expectantly to the next speaker who was to offer her story, but that lady's mouth hung open as she tried to process the greatness of the perspective she had just heard.

Here is the gift I received from Pat. Thirty years ago, a holy man told me something I have never forgotten. He said, "Remember that life is always and already perfect, and it is only the limitation of our perspective on it that ever has us experience suffering." Pat brought the truth of that declaration home to me in her story, and for that I will be forever grateful. She is a living testimonial that what happens to us does not determine our happiness or sadness. Instead, the way we choose to interpret and respond to it is what counts.

How are you doing in your life with mastering and managing your perspectives when adversity comes your way? Are you as effective as you could be in seeing the opportunity of that adversity? Are you as courageous as Pat? I know that I'm certainly not. I too often miss an opportunity to manifest the courageous view.

What if we chose to be courageous?

Pat and Wally demonstrate how to appreciate the moment with greater depth and worry less about tomorrow. Life is better when lived qualitatively rather than quantitatively. They personify the difference between not being dead and being fully alive.

Wally has passed on since the story above occurred. The process of his death and Pat's response throughout further validated Pat's courageous and inspired mind-set. She continues to live in great gratitude and love for her life.

The Comfort Trench

Imagine you are a child starting to talk. Your parents take you into a magic field with four quadrants. As you walk clockwise around the field, each quadrant has a magical quality:

- In one quadrant, as you move farther from the center, you have more control. As you move towards the center, you have less control.
- In the next quadrant, you have more interaction the farther out you walk. You have less interaction the more you move towards the center.
- In the next quadrant, the farther out you walk, the more stable you feel. The more you move towards the center, the less stable you feel.
- In the final quadrant, you feel more perfectionism the farther out you walk. You feel less perfectionism the more you walk toward the center.

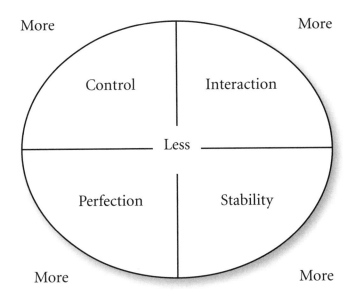

This is a metaphor for our lives. In ancient Greece, Pythagoras developed these four traits as essential human desires or needs. We are each comfortable with our own combination. Some people like more control and interaction with little stability or perfection. Others like more stability and perfection, and less control and interaction. Some who are low in one area may like a lot of control but not much interaction, a lot of stability, and a lot of perfection.

What combination do you use in your life?

Imagine that when your parents put you in this field, they attach a little garden hoe to your belt. As you walk around the magic field, you dig a trench behind you. By the time you are twenty, thirty, forty, or fifty years old, this trench is ten feet deep. Railroad ties shore up the sides and lounge chairs are down there. This is your comfort trench, your comfort zone.

You have become comfortable with your configuration of control, interaction, stability, and perfection. The good news is that this comfort zone—your set of past scripts—is the strategy responsible for whatever amount of success you currently have. The bad news is that as long as you operate within this comfort trench, your past scripts keep you from going any farther or growing any more.

One day you're sitting in a lounge chair in the Interaction section of the field and you hear a sound. You climb up the inside of your trench. Imagine that you have ten measures in each section and you were at nine. You climb up the inside of the trench and look down to two, where you see a party going on. You think, *Gosh, I want to join the party!* It inspires you to scramble out of the trench and run down there and join the party.

That is a metaphor for the fact that we are drawn out of our comfort zones when we are inspired. When we see something we want, we forget about our comfort requirements and go for it. You could say that in these times, our commitment overrides our comfort.

If you are someone with low control and you have a child who starts to run in front of traffic, you grab the child, take absolute control, and save his life because you're more committed to that child being alive than being comfortable at that moment.

When you operate outside of your comfort zone, you end up realizing that life outside is actually okay and you can grow in that arena.

The art of navigating the comfort trench is to not be limited by it but, rather, to be willing to operate outside of it. How? Inspire yourself into a state of commitment for a cause greater than feeling safe, or comfortable. You need commitment to operate beyond comfort and enter into personal growth. When you use this approach to life, you stay dynamic and fully alive.

The next tool will help you practice this.

Focus Creates Destiny

When you feel doubt, victimhood, disempowerment, hatred, anger, fear, or have a sense of scarcity, practice this Focus Creates Destiny tool, as illustrated in the following diagram.

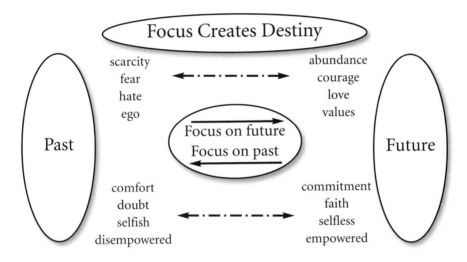

As soon as you notice you are afraid, notice where you are focusing. Are you focusing on the past or the future? Often we look with anticipation toward the future based upon our fears in the current reality and the past. We project future dark scenarios based upon our will to survive, our sense of scarcity, or our wanting to be comfortable. Our doubts about our ability to handle a situation come packaged with selfish behavior and ego identity. It disempowers us and results from focusing on the past.

Whatever the emotion you are feeling, try on its opposite.

- If you feel fearful, practice courage. Look forward and ask yourself, "What would courage or boldness make me think now instead of fear?"

- If you feel hate, ask yourself, "What would love make me think or feel now and how would it act?"
- If you feel scarcity, ask yourself, "What would abundance make me think or act like now?"
- If you feel like you want to be comfortable, ask yourself, "If I gave up comfort for now and operated as a courageous expression of my commitment, what would I do?"
- If you feel doubtful, ask yourself, "What would faith in myself, the situation, the positive outcome, or God make me think or do now?"
- If you feel selfish, ask yourself, "What would selflessness or generosity make me do now?"

You will notice that as you project a value forward into the future, an abundant, courageous, loving, values-based identity arises. It operates as an expression of commitment, faith, and selflessness. You will experience empowerment, change your state of mind, and enhance your ability to operate toward the future, giving you the power to have an impact on that future.

What Others Think about You Is None of Your Business!

Most of us develop a high degree of sensitivity to how others view us. If we become too busy living our lives through the eyes of others, we lose our own insight.

Do you become angry when someone judges you unfairly? Do you gain more confidence after receiving a compliment? These are perfectly normal reactions. If you look closely, you will see that whatever others think of you is usually more about them than you.

I once read a story about a golfer who experienced a bout of severe depression after a particularly humiliating temper tantrum on national television. He called a close friend to say good-bye. The golfer told his story, confessed that everyone in America probably saw him as a loser, and threatened suicide. At this point his friend said something very powerful.

"It's none of your business what other people think about you."

When we are excessively concerned with other people's perspectives on us, we too often use those perspectives to corrupt our own. We want to be acceptable to others, and often try to remodel our self-image to satisfy this need. This inherently undermines our trust and belief in ourselves.

We cannot do this and stay true to our own core values. When we react to other people's opinions about us, we assume those opinions are true. In fact, they are nothing more than reflections of the other person's mental filters. Often they are flawed viewpoints, filtered through their assumptions, perceptions, and biases, and projected onto you.

Overemphasizing how others view you inhibits your ability to impact your future, since you waste your time reacting to their perspective. You could, instead, use their perspective as mere input for any value it may have. Once you process it, you can once again remember your core values and move forward with courage, commitment, and integrity.

The next time you are judged, pause before you react. Ask yourself, "Is that comment about the real me, or is it just a reflection of how they perceive me? Is there any truth to their perception that helps me better practice the life values that I hold dear?"

If not, let the comment roll off your back. Don't take it seriously, whether it is a compliment or a criticism.

The Power of Choosing Your Identity

Here is another exercise to practice the next time you feel lost or afraid or too full of yourself. Ask yourself, "If I were to think of my identity right now, not as my name, my personality, my image in the world, my money, my ego, or my job, but instead as a living expression of my values, what would I think or do differently?" If you make a habit of doing this, almost like a personal mantra, you will notice over time that you will make better decisions.

You are not stuck with who you have been, who you think you are, or what the world has told you that you are. If you give yourself the power of identity choice right now and in the future, you can be an expression of your values. You will open your future to an infinite number of creative choices. Try it today and see what happens.

Creating Accountability

Do you practice accountability occasionally, or only when it is convenient or comfortable? Without accountability, how good are your intentions? How accountable are the people around you? Are your co-workers, family, and friends genuinely accountable for their commitments and actions, or do they make excuses? What does a lack of accountability cost you?

Here is how the process of accountability often works:

1. An outcome is envisioned. *I want to be slender.*
2. A commitment to reach that desired state is declared. "I will be slender."
3. A process is created to execute the commitment. "I will work out and diet every day for the next year."
4. One of two levels of accountability occur that determine whether the desired outcome is reached:
   a. Ineffective accountability: I never start the process or I don't stick to it beyond the short term.

b. Effective accountability: I start and execute the process in accordance with my commitment.

If ineffective accountability occurs, the desired outcome is not realized. Further, you undermine your ability to trust future commitments you make to yourself.

Effective accountability has the opposite result—the desired result, plus the added benefit of trust in yourself to do more of the same in the future. When you practice effective accountability, you empower yourself to get where you want to go, both now and in the future.

Accountability is the willingness and action to do what you say you will do. It is the foundation of integrity. Without it, nothing can be believed. With it, faith is created in yourself and others, and in the possibility of real progress.

Accountability has two primary components, as well as two primary forms. The two components, as mentioned above, are willingness (true commitment) and action. The two primary forms are internal (self-empowered) and external (other-empowered). Let's look at how these four elements of accountability impact effectiveness.

Of the two primary components, willingness to be accountable is the true commitment to be effective in executing actions that you conceptually commit to. Before you can take accountable action, you must have the will, or true commitment, to take that action. Without such willingness to proceed, action never takes place, other than in your own mind.

Action is relatively easy once the willingness is in place. It is the result of true commitment, and when married to the willingness to truly be accountable (not just talk about being accountable), true growth occurs. Both willingness and action must be present for positive growth to occur.

The two primary forms of accountability are internal and external. Internal accountability occurs when people operate toward an inspired outcome and "own" the accountability, independent of externally imposed consequences. In other words, internal accountability is true accountability in the sense that a person has a direct commitment to action as a representation of personal commitment and integrity. It creates long-term, continuous, powerful results that are not dependent on external support or circumstances.

Internal accountability is promise-based management of the self from the inside. It is executed as an empowered personal statement to oneself out of a commitment to integrity and the desire for true effectiveness, even in the face of discomfort.

On the other hand, we often experience people who feel that they need to be held accountable from an external source. It is a natural, hardwired script that we all have to some extent, probably beginning with our earliest relationships with our parents and other authority figures. It is an effective beginning point for adults, as with children, in the context of a behavioral management environment for external accountability to be both appropriate and effective over the short term. However, since it requires the presence of externally imposed consequences to continue, it is much less effective over time because it obviates personal commitment in lieu of fear of negative consequences.

External accountability is behavioral management from the outside through a system of rewards and consequences, thus forcing a person to act in accordance with the wishes of others. Even if we hire a person to be that external source, it has only short-term effectiveness as an approach to accountability.

Even world-class athletes can use external accountability for only so long before they must "own" the accountability internally, or they will lose motivation. In this way, external support should only be used as a catalyst to further growth, rather than as a system of long-term habit. It should also be a short-term catalyst supported by the evolution to internal accountability, which creates long-term results.

Where are you more and less effective in your practice of accountability? Answer the following questions to help you evaluate your effectiveness.[12]

1. Where do you stand with:
   - Willingness (true commitment)?
   - Action (to manifest willingness effectively)?
   - External accountability (to initiate your actions)?
   - Internal accountability (to continue your actions long term until the desired results are achieved)?
2. If you aren't effectively using all these components, how will you gain that effectiveness?

Look at these elements and adjust your relationship to them in your life, the lives of your business teams, and your relationships. Without predictable, long-term accountability, your dreams will remain mere dreams. With genuine, effective accountability, your dreams can become reality. Therefore, effective accountability is your pathway to creating any future you desire.

Results Mastery

We are trained to measure results quantifiably in terms of outcomes. As a result, we think that if we accomplish something quantifiable, we will feel successful, effective, and happy. This is often correct thinking, but not the only approach we can take to realize results effectiveness or mastery. True results mastery includes both quantifiable (measurable) and unquantifiable (immeasurable) results. Both are important.

---

[12] Go to www.integrativemasteryprograms.com/book/downloads.htm for a worksheet to help you complete this process.

Measured results allow us to assess progress in one important way. Immeasurable results, such as feelings, may be equally important to the assessment of progress. Often, what we feel matters more than what we have actually done. For example, comforting a child with a skinned knee includes stopping the bleeding and cleaning the wound. But hugging and consoling that child often matters far more over time to both the child and the person providing the hug!

The next time you face a task, ask yourself how you want to feel when you accomplish it. How would you operate as a courageous expression of that feeling? I call this results mastery.

Practice this regularly and you will notice that your state of "being" creates your state of "doing." You will be more successful and effective because you are drawing from a more holistic place based in principles, rather than personal preference and comfort.

What are you working on right now? Identify your goals? What will give you a sense of accomplishment when you finish this task?

What feeling do you want to have when you are done with the project? Is it satisfaction, a job well done, having helped someone, the ability to go play?

As you work on the project, focus on this feeling. When the project is complete, write down what feels different from having used this approach.[13]

Count Your Blessings—Literally

If you rely on others to judge what you are capable of, your future is limited by their impressions of you. If you are willing to be responsible for your own future, regardless of how others may judge you, there is no future you cannot have.

---

[13] Go to www.integrativemasteryprograms.com/book/downloads.htm for a worksheet to help you complete this process.

Do you own some electronic gizmo that you "had to have" but is still in the box? Or a book you meant to read? Or an old friend you meant to call years ago?

Are you so busy growing or protecting your overall life position that your life has become one long, tactical chess match that seldom allows you to appreciate what you already have?

Do you treat the people in your life like that unused gizmo? Are you too busy to show them how much you love them or have some fun with them?

Here is my solution: Count your blessings, literally.

Stop trying to fix the one area of your life that needs improvement long enough to appreciate the overall life that you already have. Take a vacation from responsibility, your drive for growth, and your worries about what tomorrow may bring. Instead, count your blessings as "assets" in your life and ignore the "liabilities."

For the next two weeks, look at your blessings in a deeper way. Go deeper instead of broader. You can return to defending your life-castle against the ravaging barbarians of real or imagined adverse circumstances soon enough. Write down your blessings—people, places, experiences, and things—as if you were at the end of your life looking back at your life today.

Look at the intangibles as well as the tangibles. Here are some of the blessings you may want to list:[14]

- people in your life, at all levels, who really mean something to you, and why
- places you are grateful to have been and where you will go in the next year
- your spiritual connections to your Source, your life, and other people

---

[14] Go to www.integrativemasteryprograms.com/book/downloads.htm for a worksheet to help you complete this process.

- your material assets (money, houses, cars, toys, furniture, clothes, electronics, books)
- your education and experience with growth and wisdom
- your most precious memories
- the components of your health
- anything else you can think of

Raise a glass of wine to the Source that gave you such riches in abundance. For just two weeks, refuse to feel guilty for or unworthy of your blessings, replacing those feelings with gratitude and humility.

Use this list to reform your life, to deeply appreciate what you have and where you have been, and to determine your priorities.

Barriers and Breakthroughs

The Barriers and Breakthroughs Tool is best explored using the following diagram.

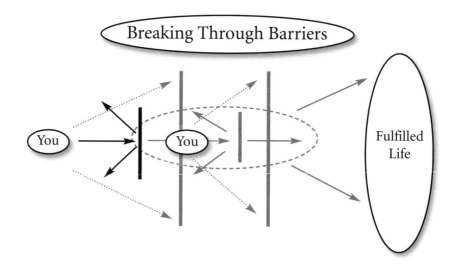

That "You" in the figure above is you, me, and everyone who has ever lived. This diagram represents us, through time, trying to achieve a fulfilled life.

As you progress through time in pursuit of a fulfilled life, you will eventually have a breakdown. Something adverse stops you in your tracks or even pushes you backwards. When this happens, you can easily grow afraid, sad, or fearful and accordingly hunker down in your past scripts, comfort zones, or comfort trench. Progress stops when you do this, however, and you must follow very specific steps to begin progress toward the fulfilled life once again. Here are the steps to take:

1. Recognize that a breakdown has occurred.
2. Since breakdowns are always caused by some sort of barrier—an external circumstance or internal state of mind—identify the barrier.
3. Create a vision that is bigger, more inspirational, and more meaningful to you than the barrier causing the breakdown.
4. Act toward that vision and break through the barrier.
5. Acknowledge the breakthrough and resume your work toward the fulfilled life you are committed to realizing.
6. When the next breakdown occurs (and rest assured, it will!), start at 1 again.

This dynamic of breakdown → barrier identification → vision creation → breakthrough → acknowledgment is repeated throughout your life's progression, which in turn creates continuous growth, the only path I know to ever achieve a fulfilled life.

Identify some of the internal barriers that stop you. Identify some of the external barriers that stop you. How can your vision help you overcome internal barriers? external barriers?

The Four-Way, One-Way Mirror

This tool can help you understand your relationship with your image in the world.

Imagine that you are standing naked in a large empty warehouse, surrounded by four mirrors, like the ones in a clothing store. You are sort of sucking it in, sticking it out, flexing your muscles, and hamming it up in front of the mirror.

This is how most of us manage our images with others. We make sure we look as good as possible. It is understandable. After all, we are socialized creatures. What we do not realize, however, is that people can see us with fat, warts, and all as we primp in front of the mirror because these four are also one-way mirrors.

The people in the world outside can look in and see us busily primping. However, they don't care because they are all busy doing the same thing with their four-way, one-way mirrors.

I use this tool to remind myself and my clients not to be overly concerned about what other people think. In fact, others are rarely concerned about us—they are busy with their own concerns. Let the four-way, one-way mirror be a reminder that what other people think of you is none of your business.

Be Here Now

Be Here Now is the title of a 1971 book by Ram Dass about his travels in India, where he learned one critically important point. I'm going to share that point with you now: The next time you find yourself in a disempowered state of sadness or fear, notice whether you are looking backwards or forwards. Notice whether your mind feels nostalgia and regret over something that happened in the past, or if you are projecting forward to a dark, future scenario. Either way, notice that this projection of the mind is creating unhappiness in your life.

Remind yourself of these three simple words: *Be here now.*

Don't "think" here now, "be" here now. Quiet your mind. Exist in the now with no past or future projections, responsibilities, or need to do anything other than feel the peace of this moment.

Practice this in your life constantly and you will see how much of your sadness, disempowerment, anger, and ineffectiveness are disillusionments created by your mind's projections. You can take refuge in the moment any time you want. Even in the darkest moments, you can dissipate negative feelings like sadness, fear, and depression instantly, by living in the present.

Looking Forward

Continue to use these tools to help you break through your barriers, wherever they arise.

In the next chapter, we will examine how to create initial commitment and stay committed when the task ahead of you seems too hard or complicated to complete.

STEP 7
Commitment

You can do what you want to do, accomplish what you want to accomplish, attain any reasonable objective you may have in mind—not all of a sudden, perhaps not in one swift and sweeping act of achievement—but you can do it gradually, day by day and play by play, if you want to do it, if you work to do it, over a sufficiently long period of time.
— William E. Holler

The seventh step solidifies commitment to help you execute the process. Are you and the others involved truly committed to executing your road map? Are you willing to experience discomfort to resolve the problem as an expression of the mind-set you have created based on your core values and principles?

If so, you are probably well on your way to completing the road map you created in Step 4. If you are floundering, you may be missing the appropriate commitment.

Commitment is taking responsibility for creating your life. If stepping outside your comfort zone causes you to hesitate, review the sections "Are You Too Comfortable?" (page 48) and "The Comfort Trench" (page 120). Comfort represents the past. When you operate within the parameters of the past, you rarely move beyond it.

Growing requires superseding comfort with commitment. The sections in this chapter will help you evaluate how you look at commitment now.

Are you committed? If not, what's in the way? Do you need to return to Step 5 (Barriers) and Step 6 (Breakthroughs to Barriers)? Is your future perfect outcome clear? Does your road map have enough structure?

Remember the Vikings who landed on the north shore of Scotland a thousand years ago? They burned their ships so no one could turn back. They had no choice but to go forward and conquer England. Warriors throughout history have put themselves in positions where no retreat was possible. That's the feeling we want to create with our commitment: "I will do all I can to make this work. No excuses, no backing down."

One way we often stop ourselves is through procrastination. Here is a five step process for conquering procrastination.

Overcoming Procrastination in Five Steps

Answer these questions for each area where you tend to procrastinate.[15]

1. Put your commitment in writing. Make it a personal and sacred act of honor.

2. Identify each task necessary to complete the commitment. Block out specific time frames in your calendar for each task.

3. Think through some negative and positive consequences for performing or not performing each task. Step 8, Monitoring, will help you develop such a system.

4. Write about what procrastination has cost you in self-esteem, effectiveness, damaging the esteem of others, and money. How will you avoid this in the future?

---

[15] Go to www.integrativemasteryprograms.com/book/downloads.htm for a worksheet to help you complete this process.

5. Don't dismiss procrastination as a small thing. Make it a major violation of your integrity and unacceptable to you. List strategies you can use when you find yourself procrastinating.

Growing Your Personal Mastery Zone

Certain people seem to have incredible power and charisma that shows through at certain moments. These people include:

- Tiger Woods in major golf tournaments
- Martin Luther King in his "I Have a Dream" speech
- Dustin Hoffman in the movie *Rainman*
- Winston Churchill during the Battle of Britain
- Your mother, when you skinned your knee as a child

These people were able to harness their focus to become their very best. Their shining moments of absolute congruity, power, and influence inspire us. At those moments, they somehow speak to our very best, too.

What we see in them is what I call personal mastery. Where is that area for you? Do you know when you are in your personal mastery zone? When have you felt it?

The key to fulfilling your purpose may be to find this zone and develop it fully. Become clear about what connects you to that power and look for ways to develop it where it is missing.

Answer these questions to explore your personal mastery zone:[16]

When do you feel like you are in your personal mastery zone?

How can you create new ways to generate this feeling more often in your life?

Note: Your personal mastery zone may not be exhibited on a large stage. You don't have to be a politician, athlete, or great orator.

---

[16] Go to www.integrativemasteryprograms.com/book/downloads.htm for a worksheet to help you complete this process.

A receptionist in a small office can have personal mastery, can create congruency and alignment in her life purpose, and can inspire others she meets, as well.

If you haven't found yours yet, begin to seek it in earnest. There is no higher secular purpose in life than to live from this place and, in doing so, to make your ultimate contribution to others. Look for it in the resources and tools in this book, the bibliography at the end of the book, or with the help of a coach, personal trainer, mentor, or spiritual teacher. Also, please visit our website at www.integrativemasteryprograms.com.

If you know where your zone is, use it more consciously, with purpose and fervor. Use it in the service of others and become who you really are.

The following tool can offer you another perspective on your choices for handling commitment.

Opportunity Triangle

Mind-Set
PLV

Strategic Priority
Leadership • Management • Coaching

Support Tools
Creative Tension • Communication Guidelines
Critical Path • Movies & Mental Models
Other People's PLV • Life Mirror Tool

Begin at Mind-Set: When you face a challenge or a problem, recognize an opportunity to practice tools of integrative mastery.

Look at the problem from the mind-set of your personal life vision or values rather than responding to it automatically from past scripts, ego, or your comfort zone.

Once there, consider the problem at the Strategic Priority level. This level involves three strategic tools:

- leadership (vision creation)
- management (process creation and execution)
- coaching (supporting forward growth)

The priority order of these strategic tools often occurs in that order. To begin, ask "What is the optimal, inspired future outcome I want for resolving this problem?" This is a leadership question that starts the process of creative tension.

Next, bring management into the mix by creating a process to move the leadership vision from the current reality that includes the steps, people, and time frames needed to execute it.

Last, consider where coaching support will be needed for you or others to successfully execute the process.

The foundational or bottom level of the triangle is a reminder that many other tools—provided in this book as well as in your own experience—are available for use. Use them as needed.

Does Conditional Commitment Count?

We said earlier that when a person commits to something, he gives his word and promises to fulfill a task to the best of his ability. Yet we often make another type of commitment, one I call a conditional commitment. We intend to fulfill it, as long as our comfort isn't violated, as long as we have time, or if no conflict or confrontation arises. In other words, although we call it a commitment, it is really more like an intention, modifiable by circumstances.

True commitment means putting your whole self into fulfilling whatever you promise. It is a sacred expression from you to the world and to yourself. No exceptions.

The reason you should visualize commitments this way is to set up your ability to trust yourself. If you know that you will absolutely follow through on your promises, you can finally declare that you have integrity. You prove you can be trusted and depended on by others.

To become unconditional with your commitments challenges you to:

- prioritize and schedule your time to be able to fulfill every commitment
- refuse some commitments and face possible confrontation
- give up the sanctuary of circumstantial excuses for the hard work of dependability

Viewing commitments this way has great power. It gives you:
- a life aligned with your truest principles
- deep and solid relationships
- a clear vision of what you want
- trust in yourself to do what you promise and significantly contribute to others
- a fulfilled and balanced life without regrets

When you declare your commitments and follow them through to completion, you can really live.

Commitment vs. Compliance

Consider whether you focus on authentic commitment or compliance. Here is how they compare:

Commitment	Compliance
Personally investing in a process or toward a desired future	Doing what is required of you by another person, external system, or external process
Personally pledging oneself to put intention and honor into supporting it	Conforming to an external set of rules or expectations to avoid negative consequences
Internal ownership to do something	Doing what others want you to do
Internal consequences, such as guilt	External consequences, such as disapproval from others

Examining these vital issues allows you to recognize how you participate in your individual life, career, family, company, community, and even country. They make all the difference in the outcomes you realize. For example, if a company has a group of employees who are committed to its success, they are much more likely to think and act in ways that sincerely express the core values of that company when dealing with its customers.

If that same company has a separate group of employees who choose whether or not to carry out company directives, they will do only what is necessary to avoid consequences for non-compliance.

In our personal lives, we are inspired and passionate in our actions to the extent that we are committed to reaching excellent results. The keys here are inspiration and passion. People who are committed are, by definition, pledging the best of themselves to the optimal outcome because it is a reflection of themselves. On the other hand, people who live lives based on compliance merely go through the motions necessary to avoid negative consequences and are far less likely to create results that reflect their best actions or thoughts, much less their personal life vision and great personal purpose.

Both Are Necessary

We need both commitment and compliance. The order in which they appear is key.

Since commitment is in the realm of personal vision and inspiration, it needs to come first. Whatever we do in our lives (i.e., our jobs, marriages, parenting or anything else), it is vital that commitment arising from passion is the first step. It empowers the entire process with the possibility for creativity, growth, and excellence.

The next step is compliance with the process that commitment creates. Too often, people and business cultures stress compliance because it is easily measurable. If commitment happens without passion, mediocrity results. The key to a successful relationship between commitment and compliance is having the intrinsic accountability of the compliance step present without eliminating the creative power of passion from the commitment step.

Most of the unhappiness I witness is due to the absence of commitment and the predominance of compliance. And most of the poor results that occur are generated by the lack of creativity and growth that comes from commitment in an environment where compliance has been allowed to dominate.

How are you doing in your various domains of life? Are you committed (inspired, passionate, creative, excited) to those domains, or do you merely go through the motions (comply with routine)? If you are committed, your life should feel like it is encompassing greater and greater possibilities and positive states. If you are complying, your life will probably feel like it is on autopilot, and perhaps running out of steam.

Power of Intention

The next time you face a challenge, ask yourself why you want a particular outcome. This will help you determine your motives and underlying personal identity.

For example, if I want someone to be fired because I think he is underperforming, that feels deliciously, self-righteously ego-affirming. He is a thorn in my side and I am going to get him fired. If I want to practice the power of intention, I ask myself, "What is my motive for getting him fired?

Let's say I want him fired because he hurt my feelings at lunch, he makes it look too easy, or he's just not working as hard as I think he should. Now I can ask myself, *What part of me has that intention? Is it my ego or my values?* This reminds me to make sure I am acting from the right identity before I identify an intention. I can correct my intention by choosing the best identity. Then I see which solution is best.

As has been said many times throughout this book, when we express our values, we manifest far greater outcomes than when we don't.

An excellent resource is Wayne Dyer's book, *The Power of Intention.* It does a great job describing why this dynamic is so powerful.

Where have you practiced ego-identified intention to your own or someone else's detriment? Where have you practiced an intention rooted in your faith, love, compassion, or integrity? Which experience would you want as your legacy? Why?

Looking Forward

The final step in our eight-step process is putting into place a system to help you monitor your progress and stay true to your road map. The next chapter will describe how to do that.

STEP 8

Monitoring

It costs so much to be a full human being that there are very few who have the enlightenment, or the courage, to pay the price. One has to abandon altogether the search for security, and reach out to the risk of living with both arms. One has to embrace the world like a lover, and yet demand no easy return of love.

— Morris L. West, *The Shoes of the Fisherman*

How will you monitor your progress and the execution of your road map? How will you ensure your commitment to move from your current reality to your perfect future? Your monitoring system is like hiring a personal trainer to keep you on your eight step plan. Your system might include other people, periodic reviews, or systems and processes. This chapter will help you put your monitoring system in place.

Review the Eight Steps

One monitoring method is to review the previous seven steps regularly. Ask:
- What is my mind-set toward my problem solving process?
- Am I objectively assessing the current reality?
- Have I created an inspirational future-perfect outcome?

- Will my road map allow me to realize the outcomes I desire?
- What are my barriers?
- What are the breakthroughs I need right now?
- How authentically committed am I to realizing the outcomes?
- Am I monitoring the process of execution and applying corrective actions where necessary?

If all eight steps are in place you are ensured successful progress toward the future you want.

How to Run Your Life or Organization

When you first get up in the morning do you ask, "What do I have to do today?"

If you are like most of us, you run your life from a "to do" list. You may keep lists on paper, in your computer, or in your head. You review the list to get your day going as quickly as possible. Sometimes this is entirely appropriate, but many times it is not.

Here is another approach.

Now	Transition	Future-Perfect
Management/ Process 95%	Management/ Process 25%	Coaching/ Supporting 80%
	Leadership 50%	
	Coaching/ Supporting 25%	Leadership 15%
Leadership 5%		Mgmt/Process 5%

Again, if you are like most of us, you run your company like the Now rectangle. You manage it 95 percent of the time and lead it 5 percent. You mostly manage behaviors of people, including your own, which is difficult and inefficient (see Promise Based Management in Step 4, page 74). You use rewards and consequences to manage behaviors in accordance with the future you want. Although that future is actually created through leadership, you only have 5 percent of your time left to think about the future. This classic formula leads to stress, burnout, and ineffectiveness.

The Transition rectangle shows you moving toward an inspired, effective, fulfilled way of operating. Here you spend 50 percent of your time in leadership, inspiring others to commit to your vision, which benefits everyone involved. The energy and passion this creates is refined through individual coaching, which enhances the individual's contribution. This leaves 25 percent of your time for an efficient accountability structure of promise management.

Management in the Transition and Future-Perfect rectangles rests on promises, not behaviors. Promises access deep commitments and allow self-managed people to hold themselves accountable. Thus, management takes only 25 percent of the time instead of 95 percent.

The rectangle on the right is the Future-Perfect state. Here, 80 percent of the time is spent coaching others based on individual talents and creativity. Leadership uses only 15 percent to maintain the vision of the inspired future that drives each individual toward a common set of goals. Only 5 percent of your time is spent on promise based management, which is far more efficient than behavioral management.

How do you run your life or organization? Are you burning yourself out with inferior results through non-leveraged management of behavior? Can you leverage yourself to actually experience fulfillment in your life and work?

Answer the following questions:[17]
1. Am I mostly managing or leading my business?
2. How much time do I spend working in the Future-Perfect state?
3. How might I integrate more and better coaching into my life and business, both receiving it and providing it?

Consider this: If a car's engine runs at top RPMs, moving 25 miles per hour in first gear, you must shift gears to take the strain off the engine and let the car move more gracefully down the road with less stress and strain.

Are *you* ready to shift gears?

The Seven Levels of Personal Mastery

You may find it useful to assess your current level of personal mastery, which ranges from completely out of touch with reality and always operating as a victim, to having total self-mastery and the ability to teach these skills to others.

These levels operate like your blood pressure. Although you constantly shift from one level to another, you have a baseline level that becomes your home base, maintained with continuous and conscientious practice. Focusing on what you want instead of what you don't want allows you to transform your life more quickly and with less pain. For example, when you focus on what is wrong with your life, job, or relationship without moving toward a PLV[18]-based solution, you operate from a more disempowered level. You are less likely to resolve the situation satisfactorily.

---

[17] Go to www.integrativemasteryprograms.com/book/downloads.htm for a worksheet to help you complete this process.

[18] Personal Life Values

Use this chart to assess where you are, and draw a circle around the level. Write the date next to it.

Level	Overview	Attributes
1	Unaware	Circumstantially react to life; victim
2	Aware; don't understand	Need clarification through dialogue and coaching
3	Understand; don't practice	Need breakthrough of ego or past-script barriers; requires faith and courage
4	Understand; practice incorrectly	Use Personal Mastery tools as weapons to judge or manipulate others, create cynicism, and increase ego
5	Understand; practice correctly with self	Begin to own the program by modeling self-empowerment and beginning to shift to a PLV-based identity instead of personality/past-based identity
6	Practice correctly with self and others	Continue to model the program and PLV-based identity, begin attracting others who want support, and receive unsolicited acknowledgement from others (abundance)
7	Train others in personal mastery	Capable of professionally practicing and training personal mastery

There Is No Automatic Pilot

Imagine piloting an airplane at 31,000 feet. The plane is your life, and you are pretty good at flying it. The sky is relatively clear, with only a few distant storms. You put on the automatic pilot, sit back, and watch. That is where the problem begins.

We practice avoiding life's risks and as we improve in the practice, we begin to grow careless. From that state, we invite risk. We try to protect ourselves from life's realities with our accomplishments, money, and reputation. Then we put our life's plane on automatic pilot to fly toward some undetermined destination that is supposed to prevent further worries.

We venture back to the galley without questioning that the plane will stay the course, maintain its altitude, and keep us safe. But while we are in the galley, we sense that the plane is faltering on its glide path. How could that possibly be?

We scurry back to the cockpit and discover that the plane has lost significant altitude. How on earth (See the irony of the metaphor?) could the automatic pilot in the "plane" of our life possibly fail? Didn't our parents and schools promise that if we developed skills and played by life's rules we could eventually put our planes on automatic pilot and all would work out?

The existential realization of all mature adults, sooner or later, is that life's automatic pilot is an illusion. We either gain or lose altitude. The control lies in our clarity, awareness, and purposeful actions with our goals in mind.

As victims of circumstance, we passively watch the plane sink into an ocean of despair. As pilots of our destiny, we determine our plane's destination, grab the controls, and take responsibility for its flight. If we do this as an expression of our personalities or egos, we fail. When we are clear about our principles and values, we gain the power to truly fly the plane.

When we realize this state, we do magic things in the sky—almost effortlessly. We have changed our identity, intentionally, and avoid self-aggrandizement in favor of personification of the universal values that serve others.

Critical Internal/External Success Factors

Answer the following questions:[19]

1. What factors have most contributed to your success? Label each **I** for internal factor (something within you) or **E** for external factor (something outside you). Some may be both **I** and **E**. Some examples follow.

2. What factors have most contributed to your ineffectiveness? Again, label each **I**, **E**, or both.

For example, a "great company" is internal (I) because you are a part of it, but it is also external (E) because other people are involved. "Discipline" is I because you are disciplined, but might be E for how other people's discipline affects you. The value of this exercise is for you to notice what skills you need, what skills others need, and which you both need.

Refer to these lists when you feel stuck. Amplify what has helped you be successful in the past and avoid anything that inhibits your success.

True Fulfillment through Conscious Risk Taking

People are either "knowers" or "learners," which determines whether they are finished growing or still open to continued

---

[19] Go to www.integrativemasteryprograms.com/book/downloads.htm for a worksheet to help you complete this process.

growth. I imagine you are a learner, since you bought this book and have read this far.

To continue to grow, however, you need to look at your perception of risk. Do you like it or hate it? Are you comfortable taking some risks, or does it cost too much when things don't work out? Will you risk in some areas, but not others?

Here is a story about using deliberate risk to enhance life.

A friend and client embarked on a thirty day adventure by himself. His undetermined destination was to be at least a thousand miles from his home. He took his suits, notebook, and laptop. His truck was full of gas. He carried no money, credit cards, or checks.

His truck travels 380 miles on one tank of gas. Within that distance, he had to help someone who would pay him enough money for gas, a place to spend the night, and a meal. He had to find a business that he could add value to, then actually provide that value. He repeated this process until he reached his final destination.

At his destination, he stopped traveling and created enough value through his efforts to earn money for his return trip, plus at least $50,000. He did all of this within thirty days of his starting date.

Why did he do this? He didn't need the money. He said, "I want to prove that it doesn't take money to make money, but it takes value to make money. I am also challenging myself to overcome my shyness."

He wanted to prove that *growth comes from risk, neutralized by information, experienced through action, created by intention.* Reduced to a formula, it might look like this:

I (Intention) + A (Action) + I (Information) + R (Risk) = G (Growth)

or

I + A + I + R = G

Further, if Growth (G) is practiced consistently, it results in a ful-filled life created by design rather than an unfulfilled life that results from mere reaction to circumstance. As a formula, it might read:

$$CG \text{ (Consistent Growth)} = FL \text{ (Fulfilled Life)}$$

$$IG \text{ (Inconsistent Growth)} = EL \text{ (Empty Life)}$$

Do you want to design your life or let circumstances and other people design it?

If you take responsibility for your own happiness and fulfill-ment, then you must also take responsibility for designing the growth necessary to create the life you desire. If you don't want this responsibility, you defer your life's outcomes to outside forces. You choose to be a victim rather than the creator of your destiny.

How can you tell if you are living a life by design or by accident? Again, look at how you perceive risk. If you fear and avoid it, you give your power to external forces. If you embrace risk with inten-tion, action, and information, you create the growth necessary to direct your life toward abundance, happiness, fulfillment, or whatever you desire.[20]

Are you curious about how my friend's adventure turned out? Amazingly, he:

- traveled more than two thousand miles
- spontaneously gave workshops to several groups
  (hotels to car dealers) on the subject of personal mastery
  and earned three meals a day and a hotel bed to sleep
  in every night
- met, befriended, and trained the board of directors for a
  Kansas bank and was compensated with exactly $50,000
  worth of bank stock

---

[20] This issue is considered in the context of things over which we have control. Spiritual and religious influences are beyond the scope of this discussion.

Where can you be taking more risk in your life? If you were to embark on a thirty day adventure, what value could you provide to earn the money you needed?

Risk Aversion/Tolerance and Growth

The other side of the risk/growth relationship is the connection between risk aversion and non-growth or stagnation. As Abraham Maslow so beautifully described in his hierarchy of human needs, we have personal security and safety as the very basic need to survive, which often manifests as risk aversion. In the face of a genuine threat that requires caution, this is appropriate. However, we must avoid being inappropriately risk averse and avoiding normal life risk.

A poignant example of excessive risk aversion is illustrated in a conversation I had with my father before he died at age ninety-five. I had asked him how he felt about his life, since he had lived to such an old age with great health. His response surprised me. He said that he felt he had wasted his life by "playing it too safe" and "playing not to lose, rather than playing to win." He explained it was too late for him to see what his life could have been had he pursued his passions rather than trying to avoid his fears.

This mind-set was prevalent for many of our parents and grandparents who experienced the trauma of the Great Depression. My father, in response to that fearsome event, gratefully took a job working for the federal government and made it a forty-year career that he never really enjoyed.

When I asked him what he would have done differently, he quickly answered, "Auto mechanic. I always loved working on cars, but I went for the security of a government job rather than pursue my passion."

Do yourself a favor. Don't end your life feeling my dad's regret. Instead, measure your risk aversion by evaluating the types of situations where you avoid taking risks and those where you are willing to take risks.

Avoidance Examples:

- "I tend to not go for the jobs I could have."
- "I tend to not ask girls out because they may turn me down."
- "I tend to not approach my boss on problems because he may get mad at me."

Courageous examples:

- "I am courageous when it comes to trying new foods."
- "I am courageous when travelling to new locations and new experiences relative to travel and adventure."

The areas on the risk aversion list are where your growth is stunted. You may be busy playing it safe and trying not to lose. Where you are risk tolerant, you tend to grow a lot and have great experiences. Any disappointments and setbacks can be viewed as new opportunities for learning and growth.

The importance of this exercise is to be more conscious and invite yourself to be risk tolerant in situations that offer opportunities for growth. Inappropriate, irrational fear can cause a person to be blind to the possibilities of his life.

Looking Forward

Now that you have completed the eight critical steps for solving problems, the concluding chapter, "Inspiration and Achievement," will give you some ideas for moving forward in other areas using this systematic toolkit for reaching empowered and fulfilling results.

CONCLUSION
Inspiration
and Achievement

The true value of a human being is determined primarily by the measure and sense in which he has attained liberation from the self.

— Albert Einstein

The eight critical steps for overcoming problems in business, relationships, and life are a time-tested process. Millions of people have followed these steps, sometimes consciously, more often unconsciously. You now have the perfect opportunity to accomplish something great with these eight steps, a chance that few people ever have. You are now conscious of them and can choose to use them to benefit your life and your loved ones, your organization, and your team. You can teach others how to use them as well.

These steps are a structured approach to a comprehensive and powerful process. They are logical, systematic, and quantifiable. You will find they are easy to understand and follow. You will experience effectiveness in overcoming problems using these proven tools and resources, as well as your own unique gifts. Inspiration will show up to help you every step along the way, including the first step, mind-set.

Commit to practice these steps with full belief and faith. An ancient Chinese book, the *I Ching* or *Book of Changes*, talks about different options we have in the face of life problems. In the introduction of one version, Wu Way says, "The *I Ching* will give you counsel and guidance from the oracle of the Universe." He says that Source gives you direction through this book. In the introduction, he states that the book is effective to the extent that you treat it with reverence, sincerity, and faith. If you are only partially of faith that it will be true, it will only be partially true. If you have no faith that it is true, it will not give you truth in the answers it provides. However, if you choose to believe in the absolute truth of the oracle (the *I Ching*), it will literally provide you true answers.

That is exactly like the eight critical steps process. These eight steps guide you to consistently and effectively achieve your goals and dreams.

Bob Proctor, author of *The Science of Getting Rich* and one of the stars of the movie *The Secret* says, "Everything you are seeking is seeking you in return. Therefore, everything you want is already yours. So you don't have to get anything; it is simply a matter of becoming more aware of what you already possess."

You must apply yourself wholeheartedly with faith, courage, optimism, and commitment, along with the belief that you will execute every step to the best of your ability.

Bringing Out the Best in Yourself and Others

What if it is within your power to bring out the best in yourself and others? What if helping other people achieve their best helps you bring out your best? Would that make for a more fulfilling life?

One of the most potent tools you have is your perception of other people in this world. That includes how others perceive you. You can choose to view the potential in others, not who they have been. We tend to view others with our own self-image in mind—whether consciously or unconsciously—and as culminations of their past. That past is expressed through their current reality, and we react to that current reality, treating it as "real."

While this is a partially accurate way of viewing people because our experiences do help create our present, it is an incomplete view. People are a combination of their past experience and their future potential. Commitment is born through our visions of the future. If you are willing to expand your perception of a person to include their past and future, you could further discover that what *determines* a person's future is his beliefs, vision, and commitment to achieving that future.

Therefore, if you are willing to impact the belief, vision, and commitment of others (which you can do by treating people as though they have already reached their future-perfect potential), you increase the likelihood that they will realize those desired futures.

How do you benefit from doing this? You allow *yourself* to be defined by your future-perfect potential, too.

Integrative Mastery

If personal mastery is about optimizing all that you can be with what you have been given, integrative mastery goes to the next level. Integrative mastery is gaining mastery beyond the self for the benefit of as many people as possible and the world as a whole. It is being fully integrated and having all parts working with all other parts. It is being quantum, holistic, and holographic.

In the realm of business, for example, you are not just a *good* leader, you are a *masterful leader* who is inspirational at the right time, in the right way. You are in the service of a higher calling of a shared vision based on your personal life vision and values as well as those of others. You do so from the highest place possible (not the ego-based self), and you do so with optimized effectiveness on behalf of all.

Personal mastery brings out the best in yourself; integrative mastery brings out the best in the whole, including yourself. It is being a great leader, manager, and coach at the same time in support of a great cause. Integrative mastery is a journey that never ends. It is the process of inspired, passionate, purposeful, effective growth that contributes to the world for a great cause, in a great way that brings us all a little bit closer to our unity.

I am fond of a word used as a salutation in India, *namaste*. The word is derived from Sanskrit (*namas*): to bow, obeisance, reverential salutation, and (*te*): to you.[21] It means "I honor the light in you. I honor that place in you that's the same as in me." It creates an awareness, a conscious recognition of the oneness between us.

Integrative mastery is the process of constantly moving toward a state of *namaste* with all other people, rather than separating, labeling, and isolating ourselves from them, which complicates finding our true selves.

The Essence

I hope that after reading this book you are willing to give up some beliefs and behaviors that no longer serve you. I hope you become more than your ego or personality. I hope that by living from your values, which connect you to the Universe, you get you more of what you want.

If you worked through this entire book, you took a challenge or situation and developed a strategic plan for changing the current reality into the desired future-perfect outcome.

What's next? I invite you to list more situations you would like

---

[21] *Oxford English Dictionary*, Draft Revision, June 2003.

to change or projects you would like to accomplish. Here are some tips:

- Remember the purpose behind your tasks.
- Set goals that accomplish something greater than survival or self-gratification.
- Define your success by the positive impact you have on other people.
- Be courageous in facing your fears and disappointments.
- Be unwavering and unconditional in your resolve to create a legacy worthy of your life.
- Worry less.
- Love more.
- Be kind.
- Trust abundance in business and relationships.
- Fight to pursue your highest purpose.
- Clarify your gift to the world and build your future around it.
- Practice faith, whatever that means to you.
- Be the "Golden Rule."
- Be grateful for what you have.
- Know that your current reality is temporary.
- Strive for a better future.

Regeneration: Refilling Your Well of Inspiration

Do you sometimes feel like your reserves are running low? When someone asks, "How are you doing?" do you answer with an automatic response? When you ask the same question, do you hope the person will not give an honest response if it is negative?

Sometimes simple prompts like this lead to real communication, then understanding and, ultimately, breakthrough.

We live in a most unique society during an important time in human history. Despite all the busy-ness of our lives, we often feel alone. When we process tasks and complete our responsibilities without restorative activities, our energy reserves (intellectual, emotional, physical, and marital) slowly run out. We find ourselves imbalanced or depressed without really understanding why.

We can get more exercise, eat right, drink less alcohol, avoid tobacco or drugs, and go to church. Sometimes those adjustments start refilling our well, but not always.

Sometimes they lack what truly restores us.

Perhaps we need to recognize and regenerate a state of "being" that is, in itself, energy creating. Perhaps we need to regenerate inspiration.

Inspiration drives effective activity. Inspirational exercise, for example, has you running or weight lifting because you are inspired by better cardiovascular conditioning or a better toned body. Without it, exercise is another "to do" on the master list. Inspiration aligns your body, mind, and spirit behind some future you wish to attain. It comes prepackaged with hope, commitment, and faith that the future is attainable. Inspiration removes doubt, fear, anxiety, and a state of helplessness.

It is empowering to operate from inspiration. You feel you can do anything. Without it, you reluctantly handle responsibilities and necessities, and forget to envision a better future.

Creating Inspiration

If you believe inspiration has to come from external forces or circumstances, you may live passively waiting for those few brief times when you are granted inspiration from another person, a sermon, a book, or a positive experience.

Perhaps it is our paramount responsibility to generate our own

164

inspiration, to create our own future. Did John F. Kennedy, Martin Luther King, Mother Theresa, or Gandhi sit around waiting for inspiration? Of course not. They did something we can do, that we have an essential responsibility to do. They *envisioned* the possibility of benefiting humanity as an expression of some great principle or value that they deeply believed in.

- John F. Kennedy stood for freedom.
- Martin Luther King stood for equality.
- Mother Theresa stood for love.
- Gandhi stood for peace.

Through their courageous decisions to take responsibility for creating a future that manifested these values, they inspired millions of others to the possibility of a better future. They overcame countless setbacks and obstacles, yet set forth inspirational repercussions that continue to this day.

To refill your well and regenerate the basic energy in your life, take responsibility for creating more inspiration.

As you contemplate creating inspiration:

- Envision a great, expanded, future that expresses a value you hold deeply and that contributes to others.
- Pursue it with deliberateness and resolve.
- Let nothing get in your way.
- Enlist others in the cause.
- Become a zealot in that cause and commit to changing the world through its benefits.

One of the things I believe and allow to inspire me is this:

Success is attainable through mere effort.
Significance, however, requires great personal purpose.
Success doesn't always lead to significance, but
significance always leads to success.

Change Your Identity to Create an Inspired Destiny

Are you the same person you were ten years ago? Probably not. Did those changes just happen, or did they occur due to some conscious decisions? In this book, you have learned that your future does not have to be a continuation of your past, and your identity does not have to depend on your experiences.

Who you "are" and how you interact with others determines how the world reacts to you. If you are kind, you tend to receive kindness back. If you are angry, people treat you with anger and impatience. If you are loving, you tend to receive love. And if you are hateful, you provoke hatred.

Both in business and your personal life, if you can choose to operate from your personal mastery zone, you can inspire everyone around you. This is exactly what the leadership experience provides you. For the sake of your employees, you become a better person than you would bother becoming if you lacked that responsibility. Don't you, as a leader, remember some experience in which you acted out of principle on behalf of another person rather than succumbing to the temptation to follow your own self-interest?

When one of your staff members makes a mistake that you yourself may have made in life (not making deadlines or telling white lies), you are a hypocrite if you act like they are inferior. However, if you become the personification of a core value or principle (honesty, integrity, etc.) and act purely as an expression of that value in your interaction with them so they "experience" that value through their relationship with you, you teach by example and give them a pure lesson in the importance of that value or principle. Their judgment of hypocrisy never arises (at least justifiably), and you have truly proven your commitment to their character development.

When you have chosen to be a personified principle in that moment, rather than your self-interested ego, you instantly become a better person for them (out of your commitment to the principle) than you would have bothered being if they weren't in your life.

Everybody wins.

This is precisely what happens when you fall in love and become a spouse or committed "other" to someone else. This is the realization that life, to be fully experienced, requires that you take on the challenge, courage, perspective and work of operating as someone more than your petty ego in pursuit of social acceptance.

We must, to the best of our ability, model the principles and values that we believe in if we want to contribute to those we love in life. That is what will support them toward their best decisions, and their most fulfilled lives.

The answer to the loneliness that most of us face, sooner or later, lies in our conscious choice of who we are.

Choose your identity going forward and, with it, your destiny.

Final Request and Exercise

This book is not perfectly written. It is, however, perfectly intended to support you in finding your unique gift, unique purpose, and power. If the spirit of my authentic desire for you to realize your fullest potential has reached you, please answer two final questions.

1. If you believe in the values-based approach presented in this book, how can you personally advance that approach in the world?
2. Who do you know that needs to learn and practice the principles and ideas in this book to be able to live a more fulfilled life?

I again offer you my personal life vision. I promise it will be your experience of our relationship, to the best of my ability.

My Personal Life Vision is a world
where all people realize their fullest potential
of extraordinary relationships and accomplishments
where integrity and honorable intentions are
courageously pursued and commonly experienced.

Namaste,
Al Killeen

∽o∾

Always you have been told that work is a curse and labor a misfortune.

But I say to you that when you work, you fulfill a part of earth's furthest dream, assigned to you when that dream was born, and in keeping yourself with labor you are in truth loving life, and to love life through labor is to be intimate with life's inmost secret:

Work is love made visible.

— Kahlil Gibran

∽o∾

SUGGESTED READING

Business/Productivity

Autobiography of Andrew Carnegie, Andrew Carnegie

Blue Ocean Strategy, W. Chan Kim and Renée Mauborgne

Blueprint of a Sales Champion: How to Recruit, Refine and Retain Top Sales Performers, William Barrett Riddleberger

Built to Last: Successful Habits of Visionary Companies, Jim Collins and Jerry I. Porras

Crucial Confrontations: Tools for talking about broken promises, violated expectations, and bad behavior, Kerry Patterson, Joseph Grenny, Ron McMillan, and Al Switzler

Dialogue: The Art of Thinking Together, William Issacs

Freakonomics: A Rogue Economist Explores the Hidden Side of Everything, Steven D. Levitt and Stephen J. Dubner

Get Clients Now! C. J. Hayden

Good to Great: Why Some Companies Make the Leap... and Others Don't, Jim Collins

How the Mighty Fall: Any Why Some Companies Never Give In, Jim Collins

How the Way We Talk Can Change the Way We Work: Seven Languages for Transformation, Robert Kegan and Lisa Laskow Lahey

Leadership and the New Science: Discovering Order in a Chaotic World, Margaret J. Wheatley

Live What You Love: Notes from an Unusual Life, Bob Blanchard and Melinda Blanchard

Love is the Killer App: How to Win Business and Influence Friends, Tim Sanders

Maslow on Management, Abraham H. Maslow

Now, Discover Your Strengths, Marcus Buckingham and Donald O. Clifton

On Becoming a Leader, Warren Bennis

Organized for Success: Top Executives and CEOs Reveal the Organizing Principles That Helped Them Reach the Top, Stephanie Winston

Personal Accountability: Powerful and Practical Ideas for You and Your Organization, John G. Miller

Real Power: Business Lessons from the Tao Te Ching, James A. and Stephen Mitchell Autry

Selling the Invisible: A Field Guide to Modern Marketing, Harry Beckwith
Shackleton's Way: Leadership Lessons from the Great Antarctic Expedition,
    Margaret Morrell and Stephanie Capparell
The 7 Habits of Highly Effective People, Stephen R. Covey
Achievement Factors, B. Eugene Griessman
*The E-Myth Revisited: Why Most Small Businesses Don't Work and
    What to Do About It,* Michael E. Gerber
The Fifth Discipline: The Art & Practice of the Learning Organization,
    Peter M. Senge

Self-Help

A New Earth: Awakening To Your Life's Purpose, Eckhart Tolle
A Whole New Mind: Why Right-Trainers Will Rule the Future,
    Daniel H. Pink
*Awaken the Giant Within: How to Take Immediate Control of Your Mental,
    Emotional, Physical and Financial Destiny!* Anthony Robbins
Man's Search for Meaning, Viktor E. Frankl
Markings, Dag Hammarskjold, W. H. Auden, L. Fitzgerald Sjoberg,
    and Jimmy Carter
*Path of Least Resistance: Learning to Become the Creative Force in Your
    Own Life,* Robert Fritz
Plato, Not Prozak!: Applying Eternal Wisdom to Everyday Problems,
    Lou Marinoff
Power vs. Force: The Hidden Determinants of Human Behavior,
    David R. Hawkins
Procrastination: Why You Do It, What To Do About It Now, Jane B. Burka
    and Leonora M. Yuen
*Quiet Your Mind: An Easy-to-Use Guide to Ending Chronic Worry
    and Negative Thoughts and Living a Calmer Life,* John Selby
Richest Man in Babylon: The Success Secrets of the Ancients,
    George S. Clason
The Alchemist, Paulo Coelho
The Autobiography of Ben Franklin, Benjamin Franklin
The Consolation of Philosophy, Ancius Boethius
The Enchiridion, Epictetus
*The Inner Game of Tennis: The Classic Guide to the Mental Side of Peak
    Performance,* W. Timothy Gallwey, Zach Kleiman, and Pete Carroll

The Phenomenon of Man, Pierre Teilhard de Chardin
The Power of Intention, Dr. Wayne W. Dyer
The Prophet, Kahlil Gibran
Think on These Things, Jiddu Krishnamurti
Unlimited Power: The New Science of Personal Achievement,
     Anthony Robbins
When Bad Things Happen to Good People, Harold S. Kushner
You Can Heal Your Life, Louise Hay
Zen and the Art of Motorcycle Maintenance: An Inquiry into Values,
     Robert M. Pirsig
Zen to Go: Bite-Sized Bits of Wisdom, Jon Winokur

Psychology/Physiology

A General Theory of Love, Thomas Lewis, Fari Amini, and Richard Lannon
*Authentic Happiness: Using the New Positive Psychology to Realize Your
     Potential for Lasting Fulfillment*, Martin Seligman
Feel the Fear and Do It Anyway, Susan Jeffers
Feeling Good: The New Mood Therapy, David D. Burns MD
Flow: The Psychology of Optimal Experience, Mihaly Csikszentmihalyi
*Further Along the Road Less Travelled: The Unending Journey Towards
     Spiritual Growth*, M. Scott Peck
Learned Optimism: How to Change Your Mind and Your Life,
     Martin E. P. Seligman
Memories, Dreams, Reflections, C.G. Jung, Aniela Jaffe, Clara Winston,
     and Richard Winston
Overcoming Addictions: The Spiritual Solution, Deepak Chopra M.D.
The Doors of Perception: Heaven and Hell, Aldous Huxley
*The Road Less Travelled: The New Psychology of Love, Traditional Values
     and Spiritual Growth*, M. Scott Peck

Spirituality

The Three Pillars of Zen Teaching, Practice, and Enlightenment,
     Roshi Phillip Kapleau
A Simple Path, Mother Teresa
Autobiography of a Yogi, Paramahansa Yogananda
Be Here Now, Ram Dass

Black Elk Speaks, John G. Neihardt

Change Your Thoughts - Change Your Life: Living the Wisdom of the Tao,
　　Dr. Wayne W. Dyer

Chuang Tzu, Tem Horwitz and Susan Kimmelman

Gandhi An Autobiography: The Story of My Experiments With Truth
　　by Mohandas Karamchand (Mahatma) Gandhi, Mahadev H. Desai,
　　and Sissela Bok

Grist for the Mill: The Mellow Drama, Dying: An Opportunity for
　　Awakening, Freeing the Mind, Karmuppance, God & Beyond,
　　Ram Dass with Stephen Levine

Journey to Ixtlan, Carlos Castaneda

Lessons from the Light: What We Can Learn from the Near-death Experience,
　　Kenneth Ring, Evelyn Elsaesser Valarino, and Caroline Myss

Make Me an Instrument of Your Peace, Kent Nerburn

Paths to God: Living the Bhagavad Gita, Ram Dass

Siddhartha, Hermann Hesse

St. Francis of Assisi, G. K. Chesterton

Stumbling Toward Enlightenment, Geri Larkin

The Art of Happiness: A Handbook for Living, The Dalai Lama

The Bible, King James Version

The Complete Works of Lao Tzu, Hua Ching Ni

The Divine Matrix: Bridging Time, Space, Miracles, and Belief,
　　Gregg Braden

The Four Agreements: A Practical Guide to Personal Freedom,
　　A Toltec Wisdom Book, Don Miguel Ruiz

The Gnostic Gospel of St. Thomas: Meditations on the Mystical Teachings,
　　Tau Malachi

The I Ching: Book of Answers, Wu Wei

The Tao of Physics: An Exploration of the Parallels between Modern Physics
　　and Eastern Mysticism, Fritjof Capra

The Tibetan Book of Living and Dying, Sogyal Rinpoche

Zen Mind, Beginner's Mind, Shunryu Suzuki

ABOUT THE AUTHOR

AL KILLEEN
President, Integrative Mastery Programs
Empowerment Mastery Guide

Author, speaker, respected keynoter, seminar leader, executive coach, and Empowerment Mastery Guide, Al Killeen is considered a pioneer in transforming clients to life and career mastery through their core values. He delivers life-changing material to shift clients painlessly towards a new, more fulfilling future.

Currently in the top 3 percent of professional business coaches internationally, Al Killeen has devoted more than three decades to studying the thoughts, actions, and habits of renowned enlightened leaders and philosophers to develop systems to support his clients. He earned his title as the Empowerment Mastery Guide by effectively supporting his clients through more than eight thousand hours of personal coaching.

A spiritual thought leader, Al has successfully trained hundreds of individuals and organizational executives in Integrative Leadership, Management, and Coaching skills using the tools and technologies of Integrative Mastery Programs. Al has worked in the pharmaceutical, finance, and mortgage industries. His 25-year history in the mortgage industry includes being president of his own mortgage company for ten years, president of the Colorado Mortgage Lenders Association (1997-98), founder/inaugural president of an 8-state alliance of mortgage associations, Rocky Mountain Mortgage Lenders Association (1997-98), and ethics chairman for the CMLA (1995).

He lives in Boulder, Colorado, with his wife of 31 years, and they have two sons.

INDEX

Order Form

Fax orders: 303-581-9081

Telephone orders: 303-544-2113

Email orders: alk@integrativemasteryprograms.com

Postal orders: Integrative Mastery Programs
                5084 Cottonwood Drive
                Boulder, CO 80301

☐ Please send ___ copies of *Soul Proprietorship*.

☐ Please send more information on coaching, workshops, and other services available from Al Killeen.

☐ Please send information on how I can hire Al as a speaker.

Name: _____

Address: _____

City: _____ State: _____ ZIP: _____

Telephone: _____

Email address: _____

    Sales tax: Please add sales tax as follows:

        Outside Colorado   none
        Within Boulder County 8.16%
        Rest of Colorado   2.9%

Shipping by air:

US: $8 for first book and $2 for each additional book
International: $18 for first book and $5 for each additional book